VOICES OVER TROUBLED WATER

Joe Rosato

Copyright © 2015 Joe Rosato
All rights reserved
First Edition

PAGE PUBLISHING, INC.
New York, NY

First originally published by Page Publishing, Inc. 2015

ISBN 978-1-68213-926-4 (pbk)
ISBN 978-1-68213-927-1 (digital)

Printed in the United States of America

Grandma Rose

I could never thank you enough for what you did for us.
I'll never forget you serving us in bed those hot fried
Meatballs wrapped in paper napkins every Sunday morning.
I will always love you.

PROLOGUE

"Tommy Lasorda couldn't make it tonight, so is this your bio? I'm going to introduce you in three minutes."

Believe it or not, those were the words that inspired me to write this memoir of a small time frame in my life. My story is true, and it covers my experiences from when I was a ten-year-old boy to twenty-two years of age. The motivation to write is something I find that must come naturally, but the right feeling didn't hit me until I heard those words mentioned above. For many years, I thought about writing my story but could never push it to its proper priority in my everyday life. Well, not until the night of October 10, 2014.

For eight years I had been volunteering as a tour guide at the New Jersey Vietnam Veterans' Memorial in Holmdel, New Jersey. One afternoon, the memorial received a call from the navy at Joint Base McGuire-Dix-Lakehurst, asking for a navy Vietnam veteran who would be willing to say a few words at the 239th birthday ball of the US Navy. Since there were only a few navy veterans volunteering at the memorial, my name came up first. I was then asked if I were willing to say a few words at the navy birthday ball held at Caesars Palace Atlantic City. I was told that I would be given a room for the night following the ball and could even bring a guest.

So I accepted the invitation and composed a short, happy birthday wish to the navy and went on my way. When girlfriend Maureen Mallon and I arrived at the hotel, we were surprisingly offered a suite that overlooked the Atlantic Ocean and were informed that the event would be held in the grand ballroom. After dressing up, we made our way down to the registration/cocktail area, which must have had five hundred place cards for those attending the event. There was a female navy chief petty officer who asked me what my name was and then informed me that we would be sitting at the head table!

All this started to roll around in my mind, and questions began to come into focus. Why were they making such a big deal over me saying just a few words and birthday wishes? Was there something missing? Had I been given the correct reason for being there?

We were seated at the head table, which included all commanding officers in the tristate area. We then noticed each place setting had a program, and while opening it, we discovered that baseball Hall of Famer Tommy Lasorda was going to be the keynote speaker for the event. I thought to myself this was going to be a really memorable night, and I looked forward to meeting such a dynamic baseball personality while maybe even hearing some juicy baseball stories.

I then was introduced to US Navy Captain Valentine, who was the person in charge of the event. I mentioned to the captain that I was really looking forward to meeting Tommy Lasorda. The captain then looked me straight in the eye and said, "Tommy Lasorda couldn't make it tonight, so is this your bio?" He handed me a short typed paragraph, which I quickly read, and nodded, affirming that it was. He went on to say, "You will be the keynote speaker, and I'm going to introduce you in three minutes."

I was completely dumbfounded, and my heart began to beat so fast that it felt like it was going to jump outside my chest. I slowly walked back to my table and gulped down someone else's full glass of red wine that felt very warm on the way down. I turned back and looked at the podium, which had a giant-size TV screen measuring at least forty feet wide and twenty feet high. My throat was now as dry as sandpaper. I obviously came to the conclusion that my short birthday wishes wouldn't cut it now. I had to quickly improvise and somehow come up with a speech that contained much more substance. I looked at Maureen then stood up and gazed over the entire ballroom. As I did, all the noise of the crowd went totally silent in my mind. All I saw was a giant room filled with young military people who, in most cases, were not even born when I served in the navy.

A voice said to me, "You have plenty of stories to express about your navy experience, which this young group of soldiers, sailors, marines, and airmen had never heard before." Captain Valentine then went to the podium and called all to stand for the Pledge of Allegiance. The captain went on to explain to the audience that Tommy Lasorda couldn't make it that evening, and instead he was proud to introduce one of their very own. Going on to read my bio, he finally introduced me.

For about twenty-five minutes I shared stories of my military life with those young guests, receiving three standing ovations along the way. Afterward, many active-duty service personnel stopped by my table after the speech and expressed a heartfelt connection with my stories.

Come read along and travel those troubled waters in my life and make that same connection with my stories. I realized then that what I had to say would resonate with all people, not only my military stories, but also the stories of my childhood that led me to be the man I am today.

CHAPTER 1

—When you're weary, feeling small.

On the afternoon on January 20, 1970, my entrance seemed a little different as I walked to the front door of our apartment. I noticed the squeaking sound of the front-door springs and the floppy sound of wobbling floorboards in the hallway. The cherry-wood raised panels that lined the hallway seemed darker than I previously remembered. As I got closer to our apartment door, I smelled the unmistakable scent of someone in the building cooking kielbasa and sauerkraut, which made my mouth start to water. I placed my key into the lock for the first time as a free man and opened the door. The phone rang, and it was my former employer's controller Marvin Morrell, who just happened to call to check in for any news of me returning home, and he couldn't believe I answered the phone after almost two years away. My enlistment should have been until March 1970, but then President Nixon had given all returning Vietnam veterans a cut if they had less than six months remaining. I will always thank President Nixon for what he did and for ending a war this country could no longer fight with resolve.

My employer before I left had been AR Traffic Consultants, based on West Thirty-First Street between Sixth and Seventh Avenue, just two blocks from Madison Square Garden. AR Traffic was one of two companies owned by Arnold Riback. The other was Capital

Parcel Service, and both combined employed about thirty employees. The company had only retail customers (department and chain stores), which performed vendor routing and freight auditing services. At that time, the customer base included Abraham & Straus, B. Altman & Co., May Co., John Wanamaker, and the Hecht Co.

Though I appreciated Marvin's call, I wanted to take off some time before returning to work, but he convinced me that if I returned on that next Monday, I would be given extra vacation time of two weeks with pay when the spring came around. I decided to take the offer and report in. But when I arrived, I found that the people I trained before leaving were now in charge, and they resented my presence and openly showed it. Not one of these people ever served their country or had any good thing to say about the Vietnam War. They all believed everything in the media as gospel. Each of them thought the war was lost and all the United States did was kill innocent civilians. I clearly saw for the first time that serving my country did not help me but instead became an obstacle in the workplace.

During the Vietnam War, our government tried to protect those who served by instituting laws that an employer had to adhere to when an employee left his job for military service. The law was full of unintended consequences and stated that the employee was only guaranteed their job back after their service. It didn't protect any advancement or increased pay that would have naturally taken place over a two-year period. So in the real world, those who used their avoiding abilities came out ahead of those who served their country, and all veterans still have a nasty taste in their mouths whenever asked what they think of the problem. Even college deferments were so convoluted that they excluded certain male students based on their subject majoring or grades while creating another inadvertent and complex system. Each able-bodied eighteen- to twenty-five-year-old had four choices during these times, and they were being drafted, volunteering, some sort of college deferment, evading and going to Canada.

On December 1, 1969, our government held its first draft lottery, which was supposed to correct the mistakes made under the old draft rules. As it turned out, if I had been 1A draft status and able to hold out just another year or so, my draft lottery number for June 8 was 366. This meant that I would never have been drafted since the highest number drafted was only 196.

Unfortunately, about two weeks after I returned to work—to make things even worse—Marvin Morrell was fired as controller, and now I had no one to verify the promise of a vacation with pay in the spring. I then made a decision that finding a better job was the only way to improve the family's finances, which now was zero dollars in the bank.

My wife, Terri, who sacrificed so much while I was overseas, had to cope with me not being at her side day after day. Each time the subject of my leaving home came up, it brought on nothing but suffering of body and mind to both of us. Preparing to leave home for two years is not an easy thing to do, especially when you're a newlywed. I had a little over a year to get my life in order before I left and always felt that there was nothing I could do to lessen the misery on my wife, Terri. After all, we only started dating a year before and really didn't have the opportunity to stop and smell the roses along the way. Terri would get so sick to her stomach just thinking of me being away and began crying so hard that she would end up hiccupping for hours. We did have a baby on the way, due in March 1970, and she had to find a doctor who would accept her for prenatal care since the navy would not treat her any longer. We were very lucky to have purchased a special Blue Cross medical plan made available to veterans being discharged without any preconditions. Dr. McCartney, who was the doctor who delivered Terri when she was born and who knew the family, decided to take her on as a patient and handled her pregnancy until delivery.

Terri was a very emotional person, and at no time did she put herself first while I was away and constantly worried about me. She always kept me fully informed of what was going on at home with both sides of the families. Through her letters, I felt as though I was part of each birthday and holiday that passed and not just a bystander. Once a month while I was overseas, Terri would send me a "care package," which included some homemade brownies, cookies, and dried pepperoni. Each and every time I opened one of her packages, my fellow shipmates would gather around, hoping I would share my bounty with them. Also in the package were newspaper articles and photos, but the most prized item was a cassette tape she would record along with family members with the sounds of those voices still ringing in my ears with unforgettable fond memories.

With the bad news of no vacation time coming in the spring, I began a new job hunt. It started off without any replies or interviews; it just felt that my résumés weren't even being read at all. The next step was visiting an employment agency or a head hunter where after reading my résumé, I was told that showing myself as a Vietnam veteran was something that had to be removed. It was explained to me that corporate America saw all Vietnam veterans as either "baby killers" or drug addicts. I very reluctantly omitted my war experience from the body of that résumé, and soon after, I started to receive replies and interviews, and I was on the way to a better future. To this day, half of me is still wondering if I sold out serving my country for no other reason but money, and the other half doing what had to be done for my family was the only good thing to do.

Our Greenpoint apartment was on Eagle Street, which was only one block from the East River that separates Brooklyn and Queens from Manhattan, and the view at the end of the street overlooked the United Nations complex across the river. Greenpoint was a neighborhood of first- and second-generation Polish immigrants that had an abandoned waterfront and old factory and apartment buildings scattered all over the community. There are two large bridges that run through the neighborhood, with the biggest being the Kosciuszko Bridge, part of Interstate 278, and the smaller Pulaski Bridge. Both spanned the Newtown Creek separating Brooklyn and Queens. I do remember at times the Newtown Creek was so polluted that it would catch on fire and you could hear explosions during the summer months. One great advantage living in Greenpoint was the fifteen-minute travel time into Manhattan, both by car and by subway. This was a big help to Terri, who remained employed while I was away at one of New York's largest law firms in midtown Manhattan as a legal secretary.

If it hadn't been for my in-laws John and Virginia Kandybowicz, I don't know what Terri and I would have done while I was overseas. One thing that made me very pleased was that they took in my wife while I was serving in Vietnam and refused to take any compensation from her. They owned the apartment building we lived in, which stood filled with relatives and low-paying tenants. The property took in just enough rents to cover costs, so John and Virginia had the expense of another relative paying a low rent. John took one of the available units on the ground floor, which had an extra half room where a future baby could sleep in and refurbished it at no cost to us. John replaced all the old worn-out kitchen cabinets with his own handcrafted units and installed a new sink and stove. The bathroom was totally updated with all-new porcelain fixtures including a tub and shower and ceramic tile floor. All other flooring throughout the apartment was also replaced with new linoleum and wood moldings.

While this reconstruction was in progress, Terri's letters to me seemed full of joy and happiness as she described the changes in detail to me while keeping me fully abreast of our new apartment. When reading those letters, I felt as though I was part of the process and not just an onlooker. Terri even spent many nights and weekends painting and wallpapering while adding her own special decorating ideas. It all turned out to be a really nice place to live for at least the short term until the new addition came along, giving us a couple of years of living space. We were only charged what a rent-control tenant would have paid, and I was always grateful to John and Virginia for what they had done financially and also for having my wife, Terri, live close to her family for moral support.

John was a WWII veteran who served in Europe in a US Army tank destroyer battalion (102nd Infantry Division) as a motorcycle scout and reconnaissance. His job description included taking advance positions ahead of tanks by keeping an eye out for the German enemy forces, and in doing so, he was awarded the Bronze Star Medal. Danger was nothing new to John, who grew up one of four children without their mother, who died giving birth to her youngest son, Allie, and with an alcoholic father while living and growing up in one of the toughest sections of the Brooklyn waterfront. The classic 1954 movie *On the Waterfront*, starring Marlon Brando and Karl Malden, perfectly described how tough and hard it was in Greenpoint during those times. Somehow, with all that against him, John still was able to do honest work as a longshoreman. All that hard work in his young years paid off along the way, and he became the owner of a bar just one block from the East River. John always said that serving in the army during WWII straightened him out while also setting him on the right path in life.

Virginia also grew up in Greenpoint and was one of six children whose father was a Polish immigrant and coal miner in Pennsylvania. He only travelled home three or four times a year to visit his family. His wife, Babcia, was not only the mother but also the family provider, cleaning homes and businesses for extra income. Virginia started working full time at the early age of twelve while also helping to care for her much-younger brothers and sister.

John & Virginia

VOICES OVER TROUBLED WATER

During the late 1950s and early 1960s, the Greenpoint waterfront lost all commerce traffic due to the containerization of cargo. Steamship companies moved their operations to other ports that had the room for mechanical handling of sea containers. There now were nothing but abandoned piers at the foot of Eagle Street, and one had to really walk tenderly to not fall into the missing planks or caved-in pier sections.

It was now a Saturday in early February 1970, and I decided to take a walk to the East River, which was a quiet place to think and reflect on how I had gotten myself into the position of trying to mold my family's future into something more worthwhile. The Greenpoint waterfront had since been cleaned up, and many of the abandoned piers are no longer there. The neighborhood is now showing a renaissance by turning old factory buildings into high-end condos. The East River remains a wide body of water that is almost impossible to swim in, and even small boats stay out of it because of the strong tides and currents. Its nickname is appropriately Troubled Water.

I had my trusty old Sony portable radio that was given to me many years before and found a safe corner to block the wind while also being a sunny place to sit and do some hard thinking. The temperature was still just above freezing, and the wind was starting to whip around in all directions. About the second or third song to play on the radio was a new one by Simon and Garfunkel "Bridge over Troubled Water," and I couldn't believe what a coincidence it was. Here I was, standing at the foot of Troubled Water, and someone had written a song about it. The opening line, "When you're weary, feeling small," willingly connected to my subconscious, making my thoughts pass into a sense of recalling my life as a young boy. As I listened to the beginning of those lyrics, my memory started to fill in, and a voice recalled a day that I would never forget. I basically decided that this time in my life and whatever came of the future, I would be prepared for anything. After all, I was a survivor and always made the best of any situation.

The voice and lyrics pulled me back to March 11, 1958, and the reason I remembered it so vividly when I was only ten years old is that day in the news, there was a story about the US Air Force accidentally dropping an atomic bomb in Mars Bluff, South Carolina. A B-47 Stratojet with a nuclear payload left for training exercises and war preparations in the United Kingdom and South Africa. The navigator mistakenly pulled the emergency release pin, which resulted in the bomb falling out of the plane. Although the bomb was not armed with the trigger, it nevertheless contained a high-explosive detonator. The resulting explosion created a crater estimated to be seventy-five feet wide and thirty-five feet deep. Today, this site still marks the location of the crater, which is just east of Florence, South Carolina, and off Interstate 95. The TV news stations kept cutting in during normal broadcasting time, and our government officials were constantly being paraded on camera, reminding us that it was safe and the fissionable material wouldn't detonate. I was totally engrossed in the story and thought of those newsreel films showing what damage an atom bomb could do and the public schools having air-raid drills with all children sitting on floors in hallways, taking the position with their backs against the walls and heads between their legs. I guess at that time schools felt they had to do something during the Cold War, but even as a kid, I knew that the force and devastation could not help us sitting in those hallways and taking that silly position.

Growing up, there were three children in our family, with me, Joe, being the oldest. My brother, Phil, known as Buster, was the middle child, and the youngest was my sister, Gerry. My parents, Phil and Ruby, purchased a house in 1954 in the small town of Wantagh, New York, which is in Nassau County on Long Island, about an hour's drive into Manhattan. My father was born in the South Bronx, New York, in a very rough neighborhood with his other eight brothers and sisters. As a kid, my dad went to what was called Reform School for those kids who needed extra discipline. One of his classmates turned out to be a famous person later in life. His named was Rocky Graziano, middleweight champion of the world. Dad served in WWII in the army's First Division and fought in the Battle of the Bulge. He ended up in life as a furniture maker and designer. My dad's war record included a Bronze Star and a Purple Heart for receiving a bullet wound in his leg. Dad always wore tan khaki pants and black penny loafers everywhere he went. He stood five feet ten inches tall with a trim build, and he had jet-black hair. My dad was considered a good-looking guy, and there were many times as a kid, I would overhear someone say, "What did he see in her?" meaning my mother, who was never considered pretty due to a broken nose that left a flat bump at the bridge of her nose and who had a way with curse words that always placed her in the gutter.

Rocco and Maria Rosato were my father's parents, who were both immigrants of Italy. My grandfather Rocco was blind from an early age due to a genetic eye retina disease that was passed on to half of his children and their children, but luckily my father did not have the disease, and it was not passed on to me or my siblings. In the early years, my grandfather Rocco was in the ice-delivering business with a horse and wagon. He could carry one-hundred-pound blocks of ice at times up four flights of stairs because the horse had the route memorized. He was able to support his large family without taking any social assistance and was very proud of it. This worked out well for years until the horse died one day and Rocco could not continue his business any longer due to his blindness. He then began to sell newspapers at a newsstand on Third Avenue in the Bronx just a short walk from home.

My mother was born in Manhattan's little Italy section, and my mother's parents, Filippo and Rose Del Prete, settled a few years later into a home in the Gravesend section of Brooklyn, New York. My mother was the oldest of four children, and she stood at four feet ten inches tall but had a mouth to make up for her size. My grandfather Filippo was in

Mom & Dad

the Italian groceries business with his routes covering Long Island, Connecticut, and New Jersey, for which he left very early in the morning and returned home in the late afternoon. His preference for vehicles was Willys Jeep wagons, which allowed him to go out in bad weather situations and serve his customers.

That same afternoon on March 11, my father called my mom and told her that he had to work another late night to catch up on projects in his shop on Second Avenue and Fifty-Ninth Street. It was an antique and interior design store called Bari Galleries, which he named after Bari, Italy, where my father's side of the family came from. The shop was at the foot of the Fifty-Ninth Street Bridge, also known as the Queensboro Bridge and now known as the Ed Koch Bridge. The bridge connects Manhattan and Long Island City, Queens, and crosses over what was called Welfare Island, now called Roosevelt Island, and the East River's Troubled Water. Final construction of the bridge was completed and opened to the public on March 30, 1909. Today there is no reminder left where that shop stood since all the buildings on that block were demolished in the late sixties to make room for the Roosevelt Island Tram.

My mother was taken aback by what my father's motive was for being late again. She also worked on sewing at home to help out, making slip covers, curtains, and drapes, and was considered an expert in her own right. A few hours later, my mother decided to dress my young sister and asked my brother and me to also get dressed; we were going to make a surprise visit to Daddy at the shop.

We arrived at the shop at about 8:00 p.m. and parked in front when an open parking spot became available. The shop was blacked out with no lights on and locked from the inside. It seemed that my mother pounded on the door for a half hour without my father coming out to open it. There was a pay phone off to the side, so my mother called the shop, and there was no answer. Apparently, my father wouldn't pick up. Then all four of us walked down Sixtieth Street and found my father's green 1950 International Metro step van parked in its usual place. My mother then realized something wasn't right, and she started to panic. We walked back to Second Avenue where my mother noticed a cop directing traffic at the foot of the bridge and summoned him to come over. She explained to the cop that her husband was inside and wouldn't answer the door. The cop walked over to us, took out his night stick, and started knocking on the metal frame of the glass door, yelling out, "This is the police! Open up the door!"

The store had two levels with the street level used for displaying various types of antiques, including small items such as vases and lamps to much larger sofas and dressers. Upstairs was used as an office area and workshop, which overlooked the entire store from above with a clear view of Second Avenue through the glass window wall. The store layout allowed work to be done upstairs and at the same time keep an eye on the store below when a customer walked in.

By then, it had started to rain, and all of a sudden a taxi cab showed up in front of the shop and doubled-parked on Second Avenue. The shop's lights began to come on starting in the rear of the building on the balcony level, and then my father showed himself at the door and signaled to the taxi driver to open his door. A beautiful, tall, sleek woman with a scarf over her head ran through the doorway directly into the taxi and locked the door. She then looked straight at me through the taxi window with larger-than-life eyes showing both a look of surprise and sorrow when our eyes met. My mother rushed to the taxi and tried to open the door but couldn't, and then she decided to hold on to the door and not let go. The cop then forced my mother's hands loose, and the taxi swiftly pulled away. The rain was now coming down harder, and the cop now convinced both my parents to take their arguing inside the shop and off the public sidewalk, and he also told them that if he were called back, there would be arrests made.

The three of us kids were lying down on couches surrounded with all kinds of antique items in the shop, and both my brother and sister were sleeping and I was filled with terror, hoping and praying that all of it would somehow end well. Both my parents were yelling at each other, and as a ten-year-old, I started hearing some accusations and demands that didn't make sense to me then but do now. My father kept answering my mother's "How could you do this to me?" with a strong outburst of when he was in WWII, serving in the army, his sister Betty would write him, saying that my mom wasn't being loyal to him and was fooling around with other men, and it was now his turn and she should shut up. My father's face and voice were filled with anger, and he continued cursing while he finally locked up the shop by closing all the lights.

The arguing now moved out of the shop and back on to Second Avenue and down into the green Metro step van on Sixtieth Street, which was loaded with upholstered chairs and couches waiting to be delivered. This gave us kids another place to settle in for another round of arguments filled with yelling and screaming. Time was running late and it must have been about midnight, and I could hear both their voices starting to wear out and beginning to go hoarse. I couldn't wait for it all to stop so we could once again return to a normal family. But that would never happen, and my future would tell the tale.

Suddenly my mother woke up my brother and carried my sister and told us, "Come on, let's go," and we four stormed out of the step van while Mom yelled out to my father, "Since you don't want these kids, I'm going to leave them on the bridge." Then she grabbed our hands and ran to the car and jumped in. Mom started the car and drove around the block a few times before heading over the Fifty-Ninth Street Bridge. I looked back through the rear window of the car for my father and couldn't find any sign of the step van headlights behind us. I started to wonder if Mom was really going to leave us on the bridge, and all of a sudden my body began trembling. About halfway over the bridge, she slowed down and let other vehicles pass by. She then pulled over to the side and grabbed my brother and ordered me to get out of the car and follow her. I stood shocked and paralyzed. My legs wouldn't move, and the trembling got worse. All I could think of was, *Why me? Why now? What have I done to deserve this?* Taxi cabs were speeding by, honking horns and flashing their headlights, but no one ever stopped to see what was going on. Then Mom reached out and again grabbed my hand and pulled me behind her and my brother, and we head onto what I thought was a walkway. There was a railing that I took hold of while also holding on to my brother. I tried again to pull back, but Mom was determined, and she won the battle. She then told me that we both should stay there until my father came to get us and started walking away. I cried out to her not to go, but it all fell on deaf ears. She left us both on the bridge and pulled away with my sister in the car. I looked down at the rushing water below and watched barges swiftly moving downriver and the currents swirling around and around with lights of amber, green, and red reflecting from the bridge. Tugboats were sounding horns and pulling what looked like massive barges as long as football fields, and car headlights were coming and going in all directions.

I was shivering and wet right through my clothes and couldn't help but think what if my dad didn't care where we were or he couldn't find us? The rain now started to slow again to a slight drizzle, but the temperature was frigid. Looking downriver, I wanted to cry but couldn't come to tears. A voice was telling me to be tough and not show my feelings because all the crying in the world would not help.

A ten-year-old should have been thinking of the Mickey Mouse Club instead of hearing voices repeating over and over that his parents didn't love or even want him anymore. Every time I heard a horn sound, I thought it was my dad coming to the rescue, but it seemed that over a dozen times, it was nothing but false alarms. I started marking promises to God that his help now would allow me to never again ask for anything again as long as I lived. After at least fifteen or twenty minutes of total terror, a funny horn started to sound in the distance, getting closer and closer. That green Metro step van never looked so good when it came close, but it then slowly passed us. I yelled out at the top of my voice for it to stop, and it did. I then saw the white backup lights on and realized my dad either saw or heard us and we would be safe. The passenger side sliding door opened, and my father ran out and crossed over to the walkway where my brother and I were standing clinched to the handrails. Dad hugged the both of us and took us into the safety of the step van and told us we were heading home. There was no other conversation in that van for the entire ride home. Our clothes were wet, and Dad gave us a blanket to help keep us warm. That old International's heater wasn't so good, but the warmth of the blanket felt good as I started to dry off, and I finally fell asleep.

The next morning, my father woke us up already dressed for work and asked my brother and me if we had seen Mom. I answered no, and we both were then asked to get dressed. My mother must have been home that night since my sister was there. Shortly thereafter, the four of us started to leave the house without my mother, and my father put us in the family car, which was a white 1956 Cadillac convertible. The Caddy had a black canvas top with red leather interior that I can still smell today. Mom and Dad had purchased the used car just two weeks before and traded in their 1952 Buick Special. It was my dad's dream car, and he couldn't wait to drive it with the top down when the weather was warmer.

My dad shortly announced that we were going to be dropped off at my grandmother Rose's in Brooklyn and he would then go to work. Dad drove about as far as the entrance to the Southern State Parkway just a few miles from home. I was sitting in the backseat, when I began hearing whispering from behind me. I got on my knees and looked down into the space where the convertible top folded into when in the down position and saw my mother balled up and hiding. She was whispering to me not to have my father know she was there, but Dad took a glimpse in the rearview mirror and noticed me talking to someone. Suddenly he pulled over to the shoulder of the road, and the car came to a stop. My dad opened the door and bent over the seat and found Mom hiding. He pulled her out, and they once again started arguing for a short time, since I'm sure they had nothing else to add from the

Me, Buster, and Gerry

night before. Mom reluctantly got into the backseat, and we returned home, where Dad got into his step van and headed back out for work without saying another word.

I still to this day don't know where my mother went after dropping my brother and me off on the bridge and what would have happened if my father never came and found us. Did she hang out and make sure we were safe, or did she just go home and leave it to my father? I'll never know for sure, and years later, whenever I brought up the subject, she didn't want to discuss it and would walk away tight-lipped.

I later found out that the woman in the shop with my father that rainy night was a well-known model and spokesperson for Scotties tissue. She appeared in television commercials and magazine ads, and her name was Joanne Kelly. The Scotties commercials were constantly playing on all TV channels since Scott Paper was a major sponsor at the time. Whenever my mother was in the room and a Scotties commercial appeared, she would take a fit and threw whatever was handy at the television. Mom also used some language at that time that didn't register with me, and she also didn't care who was around and seemed to show more anger when she had a larger audience. I regularly had dreams about Joanne Kelly, and her face would constantly appear with those larger-than-life eyes over and over even when I would never again see her in person. That short glimpse into her eyes on that night was enough in my mind to last a lifetime, and each dream never had a good ending. I still to this day can exactly recall what she looked like and those raging eyes that always left a lingering impression.

My brother and I were only sixteen months apart in age, but it seemed that Buster had an introvert personality. His size was much smaller than mine, and his physical abilities were far from my own. Buster started shortly afterward having his own more severe nightmares that would also cause him to actually jump out of bed and start running away in his sleep, yelling and screaming at the top of his voice. As the years passed, it seemed that his dreams were getting worse and placed him at risk of hurting himself and others. During these bad dreams, I would also have to jump out of bed and stop him from running into furniture and doorways that were in his path. It seemed to me he was also traumatized by that night on the Fifty-Ninth Street Bridge, and this was his way of showing all that exploding fear in his subconscious memory.

> The oldest and strongest emotion of mankind is fear, and the oldest and strongest kind of fear is fear of the unknown.
>
> —H. P. Lovecraft

CHAPTER 2

—When tears are in your eyes, I will dry them all.

My parents did not get along very well after that intensely explosive night over Troubled Water, and before long, they decided to place the house in Wantagh on the for-sale market. At this time, my father showed what I sensed as very little remorse for his actions while his presence with the family became more infrequent as the days and weeks passed. There were periods when more than a week would elapse with no sign of my father or even a phone call. I could feel and see the total frustration in my mother's face and in her actions. Mom would unsuccessfully try to call everyone my father knew including my aunts and uncles and ask them if they saw or heard from Dad. Their replies always gave Mom no hints or clear answers of his whereabouts. During these frightful days of my father's unexplained absences, I experienced the feeling that somehow it was my fault in addition to us kids now being a burden on Mom. The Bari Galleries business was also very much affected by Dad's absences and slowly started to fail. Our house was sold under market value in what appeared to be a very fast time frame, which I'm sure was a direct result of Dad not being around very much. As soon as the sale on the house closed, Dad left the family and moved in with Joanne Kelly and never returned.

Over the next ten years of my life, my father made no more than five visits to see his three children. My mother tried to set up an apartment in the Howard Beach section of Queens, New York. The building faced the Belt Parkway with just a short ride to Idyllwild Airport, which is now JFK Airport. Road noise from the parkway was hard to get used to at night, and the rumble would shake the windows. Mom felt comfortable in Howard Beach since she had a best friend named Lillian, who lived only ten minutes away with her own family. The idea of nurturing three young kids and a Scottish terrier named Topsy in an apartment without any financial support from my father was short-lived. My brother and I were registered in school at Howard Beach but only went for a two-week period before Mom decided to take all three of us and Topsy to our grandma Rose in the Gravesend section of Brooklyn, New York.

Gravesend was an area in the southern part of Brooklyn, which was separated from Coney Island by a small body of water nicknamed Perfume Bay, which didn't smell like any perfume I knew of in the summer months. It was so polluted that any fish swimming in it would die, and the smell would be even worse. Each year in the late spring when blue fish began their migration, thousands of mackerel would be chased by the blue fish and get caught in Perfume Bay and die, creating a stink that permeated for miles. Most of the subway lines that crossed the small bridge over to Coney Island had to stop for a red signal, causing passengers to sit and wait over the putrid stench. Gravesend acquired its name from the Revolutionary War and Lady Moody, who was a local tavern owner who made sure that all colony soldiers killed were properly buried. The British forces placed a bounty on her head, dead or alive, and the graves of those soldiers are now rightfully called Gravesend Cemetery. Lady Moody Square was where she lived.

My cousin Phil "Chick" Del Prete had already been living with Grandma Rose. He moved in after the death of my grandfather Filippo Del Prete a couple of years before. Grandma Rose was a small person, standing only four feet three inches tall. And regardless of what season it was, she always sported a cotton floral-print housedress with flesh-colored cotton stockings rolled up and over her knees and black three-inch-thick-heel shoes. The same style of shoe she wore always reminded me of nun shoes. Her winter digs only changed by adding a black sweater over the housedress with only the top button buttoned.

Chick was the son of my uncle Curly and aunt Dolly and was two years older than me. He had complete run of the house while my grandma Rose couldn't do enough for him and must have really enjoyed the company after my grandfather's death. Being two years older than me gave him the advantage of size and ability, especially during the early years. A few years prior to moving in with Grandma Rose, Chick and I played musical instruments. The family would force us to play songs together. Chick played the guitar while I played the accordion, which I detested and only played because my mother demanded it of me. It was a full-size accordion that had a case included, which together weighed almost as much as I did. Carrying my books while lugging an accordion twice a week on a school bus in Wantagh wasn't too easy for a second grader.

Grandma Rose was a housewife who owned two homes next door to each other with only Social Security benefits as income, so she really was house-poor. My two uncles and aunts lived next door. Curly and Dolly and Sal and Cathy were charged rents that just covered expenses. But now there were three more children and a dog in Rose's life, even though my mother promised that our stay was only short term. Once she found a job and another apartment, all four of us would move. Within what seemed a few weeks, my mother's presence with us kids was less and less. Finally, she would make an appearance many months apart and showed up unannounced if at all. Mom became a barmaid, and her first job was in a bar and grill in Atlantic Highlands, New Jersey, which is a small town on Raritan Bay, just a short drive to Red Bank, New Jersey.

Mom's new job turned out to be a bad episode for me and my siblings. After just a short time, she decided to move the three of us once again with her to a two-bedroom motel room owned by her boss, which had a small kitchen and sitting area. It was the summer of 1959, the motel was right next door to the restaurant/bar, and Mom would take my sister with her next door while my brother and

I had to stay in the motel unit. The summer heat was overwhelming since we didn't even have a fan, so my solution was to sit in Mom's parked 1957 turquoise-blue-and-white Chevy Bel Air coupe all day, playing the radio with the windows down and occasionally running the engine to charge the battery. I started to listen to the top-forty radio stations of the day and preferred WMCA with Joe O'Brien in the morning, Harry Harrison in the afternoon and Scott Muni at night. Some memorable songs being played were "Dream Lover" by Bobby Darin, "Mr. Blue" by the Fleetwoods, and "Sleepwalk" by Santo & Johnny.

The beach was just a half block away, but we were not allowed to go. Only one time I remember Mom took us to the beach on her day off. This beach had a giant water slide the height of a house that hooked up at the end and would throw the slider up in the air about ten feet and land in four feet of water. It was the greatest ride I ever had, and I enjoyed running up and down that slide the entire day. Mom never took us back to the beach even though I would request it many times. Her love life started to interfere with us kids living in that motel unit, when she started to bring home boyfriends in the night. It would wake me up, and I would have to pretend to be sleeping and listen in the darkness of night. At twelve years old, I knew enough and had learned the lessons of life, so I started to recall those words my father implied to defend his cheating. Had they been true?

On one of the holiday weekends during that Atlantic Highlands summer, Uncle Curly, Aunt Dolly, Grandma Rose, Chick, and my cousins Sal and Roseann came to visit. The sleeping arrangements were tight, to say the least, and

Chick

it was a great feeling being all together again. By the second day of their visiting, I learned that it was not just for fun and relaxation but instead checking out our living conditions. Grandma kept asking questions about what we ate and did during the days and nights and how we were being treated. I never told her or anyone else about mom's boyfriends visiting.

Curly, Chick, and I went fishing at a place called Frank's Pier, which charged one dollar per person to fish all day. The location was recommended by some locals who told us the waters were filled with fish and they were biting. It turned out to be the best fishing day of my life, and we caught a large burlap sack full of fluke with each fish being larger than normal. Grandma Rose and Aunt Dolly fried the fish in whatever pots they could find, and I remember the smell saturating the grounds of the restaurant and motel. It all made for a delicious dinner that night with still enough for them to take back on ice to Brooklyn. I didn't want that weekend to ever end. When it did, I really had a hard time holding back the tears because I didn't know when I would ever see them all again. Chick and I bonded during those days, and my uncle Curly would say, "You guys act just like brothers." When my uncle's green Mercury backed out of the old motel driveway, you would have thought it was an execution taking place by the look on my face. I waved good-bye, and in the blink of an eye they were gone, and we three kids were again all alone.

However, in an answer to my prayers and to my amazement, within just a few weeks, my mom decided to take us back to Grandma Rose. She dumped us off without saying a word or giving a reason. I felt as though I was resurrected back into a normal lifestyle even if it didn't include my parents, and I was very happy to be back with Grandma Rose. Looking back on that visit from Curly, Dolly, and Grandma Rose, I now see that it definitely had a purpose, and the outcome was a good one.

We three kids were basically parentless now and cared for by Grandma Rose without any monetary support from either my father or mother. When I look back, it was the best of times for a child, and she gave us unconditional love without asking for anything in return. I owe everything to Grandma Rose. She was able to teach me all I know in spite of her never being educated past the fourth grade. She possessed a special gift of knowledge. Her ability to keep us kids as a family and have the safety, the shelter, and the love needed to survive in a world of turbulence was amazing. There wasn't a day in my life living with my grandmother that she didn't say "Grandma loves you," and in the middle of each night, she would get out of bed and tuck Chick, Buster, and me back under our bed covers. Each morning at 6:00 a.m., you could hear her ironing our clothes, and as a special treat on Sunday mornings, she would bring fresh, hot fried meatballs wrapped in napkins to our beds. Waking up to the aroma of crusted hot meatballs and then biting into one, causing the hot juices to gush out, is one of those unforgettable moments that still flashback for me every now and then.

Grandma Rose was born on a farm in Saugerties, New York, and spoke only Italian with her siblings and parents and had a broken English accent when she spoke. Saugerties is close to Kingston, New York, on the banks of the Hudson River about seventy-five miles north of New York City. Most people that spoke to Grandma Rose for the first time thought she was an emigrant from Italy because of the accent. She was married at the young age of only sixteen and moved from her parents' farm to an apartment with Grandpa in the Little Italy section of Manhattan, New York. This was also where my mother and her two brothers (Curly and Sal) were born. My grandparents then purchased a house on West Tenth Street in Gravesend Brooklyn, New York, when there was nothing but potato farms and Coney Island just two miles away. New York City's subway system was then extended to

Grandma Rose

include this new open land area of Brooklyn to a large influx of residential building.

In the late 1940s, my grandparents (Filippo and Rose) purchased the house next door and then converted their building to a two-family and the other to a three-family residence. My parents in the early fifties lived in the basement apartment next door to my grandparents with my brother Buster and me before my sister Gerry was born. Grandpa Filippo now had fulfilled his dream of having most of his children and grandchildren living all together as one big happy family, or so he thought. The only one of his children who didn't live in any of the two homes was my aunt Anna and her husband, my uncle Auggie. Aunt Anna was first married to my uncle Joe Musumeci for only two weeks when he was killed on September 5, 1946, in a plane crash while serving in the US Army just after WWII ended. I was named after my uncle Joe, and I still honor him in spirit each and every day for making the ultimate sacrifice for his country.

When Grandpa Filippo suddenly passed away in 1956 from colon cancer, the family went into turmoil because they lost the patriarch who held the family together and set the rules along the way. Without him being around, arguing between the three families was common. One day there was a major blowout, and my father ended up punching Uncle Sal and knocking him out. At this point, my parents rushed out to purchase the house in Wantagh, New York, and both vowed to never return, or so they thought.

Grandma Rose's house was two homes away from an old mansion that was vacant and abandoned, and all the kids on the block called it the haunted house. It had a high chain-link fence with barbed wire at the top and was used as a dumping place by other residents. That old house was being demolished to make way for new homes and was infested with rats that terrorized the neighborhood. About nine months after we moved in with Grandma Rose, a friend of mine named Tubby, who lived across the street, walked through the driveway and down the steps to our back door, something he did every school-day morning, and we both then would walk to school together. This same morning, as he opened the door, a large rat about the size of a small cat ran into the kitchen and behind the cabinets and into the walls of the house, and we now had our own rat problem.

Grandma shortly started noticing entire loaves of bread were missing with only the empty bags left behind. In addition, we began hearing something running inside the walls and ceiling or the basement living space. We were all freaking out at this time and had to find a solution. Both my uncles came to the rescue with Sal being the first who thought poisoning was the best solution, so he found a rat poison that actually smoked when the can was pried open. The poison was spread on pieces of bread and placed inside cabinets and the kitchen oven. Each morning, all the bread would be gone, but there was never any sign of any dead rat, so it was repeated each day for about a week. At this point, both my uncles agreed that large rat traps would do the trick so they placed the largest traps I ever saw with provolone cheese as bait. That very first night, at about 8:00 p.m., we all were watching TV and heard a hard snapping sound that sounded like a gunshot. We then started to hear a rumbling sound in one of the cabinets that kept on getting louder. Someone went out to knock on both my uncles' doors, and they came running next door and downstairs. The rumbling sound kept on going, so we had to open that cabinet door and face what we caught.

Uncle Curly decided that he needed a weapon when the door was opened so he would be ready, so he went to go get his gun next door. He returned with a bolt-action .22-caliber rifle and took hold of a position over the kitchen table where he would have a steady aim. I was chosen to be the person to open the cabinet door and stood far away, reaching over to grab the handle, and on the count of three I opened the door. The rat leaped out about four feet from the cabinet and landed on the kitchen floor with both of its rear legs caught in the trap, which no one ever expected. Our dog, Topsy, went crazy and ran to the screen door and pushed it open and ran away, barking and howling. We all jumped back, and Curly's aim was now not on target, but he started to fire about twelve rounds from the rifle anyway. The rat was hit about four or five times with all those bullets passing right through its body and into the wall along with the missed rounds. There was blood all over the wall, floor, and cabinets, and the rat finally showed no signs of life. Topsy couldn't be found for three days, and when we did find her, she had to be dragged back into the house. She correctly feared there were more, and she wanted no part of it. Grandma's house, along with other neighbors', had additional smaller-rat issues for about six months until they were all exterminated or relocated somewhere else.

We three kids were now settled in with Grandma Rose and registered in school at PS 248, where I started the fifth grade. This was now the second time I attended PS 248; the first time was during kindergarten and the first grade before we moved to Wantagh. At first, all seemed well at Grandma Rose's except when my uncle Sal came downstairs and complained about us kids living there. Uncle Sal hounded Grandma Rose every day, it seemed, saying we kids didn't belong there and should be sent to a home for adoption if my mom didn't want us anymore. It wasn't a good thing to hear when you're a kid growing up. Uncle Sal yelled it out for years and didn't care and said it even when we kids were present. Grandma Rose would argue with my uncle Sal over the years, and she would say that he didn't understand and that it wasn't costing him anything, so he should keep out of her business. She said we kids were staying no matter what. Uncle Sal always felt that I had to earn our keep, and since I was the oldest, he constantly found things for me to do around either house, whether it was painting, sweeping, hosing, or shoveling snow. I had to do whatever he said and realized in my younger years that if I didn't, I would be sent to a home for orphans.

On the other hand, my uncle Curly was much more supportive, and I think he and my aunt Dolly really felt sorry for us kids. I spent many weekends over the years during the summer going fishing and crabbing with my uncle Curly. He would always include me in these events. Aunt Dolly would always pack me a lunch. These early-year fishing/crabbing trips included Chick and his brother, Sal, along with me. My brother, Buster, wasn't interested in any sports or at least didn't show it and was at that time a homebound kid.

Me & Uncle Curly

Our first favorite fishing place was Jacob Riis Park in Queens, and for crabbing, it was off the Jamaica Bay Bridge, also in Rockaway Queens. Jacob Riis Park was an area across Floyd Bennett Field Naval Air Station in Jamaica Bay, just a stone's throw from JFK Airport. My cousin Chick and I both bought and shared the cost of purchasing a crab pole and added extensions that made it about twenty feet long. We were really good at crabbing, and the pole allowed us to walk along both sides of the bridge, scooping up crabs right in front of people, using drop traps. Uncle Curly stayed with the fixed crab traps in one location, and Chick and I would unload our catch with each roundtrip of the bridge. On a good day, we would come home with at least a bushel full of nice-size crabs, and neighbors would come over and gaze at our bounty. On a bad day, when there were no crabs caught, my uncle Curly would stop at a fish market and purchase some so he wouldn't have to show up empty-handed. Aunt Dolly wasn't fooled and figured out the false catch. She stared at her husband with dagger eyes and would say, "You could have stayed in bed on this your day off and saved money not going," but she knew he was as happy as could be when crabbing or fishing. Chick and I spent a lot of time together, and we even had the same friends. Chick became closer to me than my brother, Buster, and my uncle Curly would repeat saying we acted and stuck together like brothers.

Both my uncles had a source of extra income, but for Grandma Rose, it was extra income to put food on the table money. They occasionally participated in receiving stolen property from a guy called Scotty (Scotese), who would show up at all hours of the night and sell my uncles various items, such as auto tires, cigarettes, and television sets. Scotty had master keys for every new car's trunk and would enter car dealerships under the darkness of the night and open the trunks and empty out the contents. Whatever he found, my uncles would purchase from him and resell to neighbors or customers on their grocery routes. Grandma Rose was the first to be awakened by Scotty knocking on her window, and she would then call my uncles to come down. Living in that Gravesend neighborhood, I realized from the beginning that most of the other families also had something on the outer limits of the law going on in one way or the other. Scotty was a generous person to us kids by giving items to Grandma Rose that she could use to help us out. We kids had clothing given to us by Scotty, which I can't imagine where we would have gotten the money to purchase them.

There was a time when Scotty showed up with a load of remote TVs, which we had never seen before and most people didn't have. The TVs were sold to neighbors, and my uncles gave one to Grandma Rose and also kept one themselves. What no one realized was that the remote mechanism used an ultrasound device to change channels and shut off and on. Apparently, when each neighbor changed the channel or shut off their TV, it would affect their neighbors, thus causing havoc on the block. It took some time to figure it all out, so my uncles had to refund certain neighbors and sell those TVs to distant customers. After a few years, the Scotty visits slowed down to a trickle, and eventually he opened up his own secondhand store in the neighborhood and sold directly to the public.

There was this little coffee shop at the end of the Jamaica Bay Bridge that we were very fond of, and it also sold bait and tackle. Chick and I nicknamed the place Tavern on the Green after the famous restaurant in New York's Central Park, where rich and famous clientele would frequent. On one Sunday morning in September 1960, when Chick and I were leaving Tavern on the Green with our coffees and giant crabbing pole, we crossed over the road and walked toward the shoreline of a beach at the end of the bridge. There was a flock of seagulls gathered together and what seemed like a stuffed dummy wearing a green uniform and holding a pick stick and a canvas trash bag lying on the sand. As we both walked a little closer, a strange odor started to fill the air around us, and as we walked even closer, the odor became stronger. I was then about only three feet away, and it suddenly came to me that this was a dead person and the gulls were about to have breakfast. We both ran as fast as we could back across the road and into Tavern on the Green, where a man behind the counter yelled to us to stop running. We were out of breath and tried to explain that we found a dead person on the beach across the road. At first I didn't think the man behind the counter believed us, but the looks on our faces must have changed his mind, and he called the police. He then told us to go back over to the area where the body was and show the police where it was when they arrived on the roadway. We later found that the dead man was a US parks employee who was reported missing by his family that Friday night when he didn't return home after work. The police later informed us that he must have had a heart attack and died right where we found him on Friday afternoon.

By the mid 1960s, we started to venture out and travelled in my uncle's dark-green 1953 Mercury coupe all the way to the Jersey Shore at Pelican Island, which was between Toms River and Seaside Heights, New Jersey, right in the middle of Barnegat Bay under the Toms River Bridge. Uncle Curly didn't give up on Riis Park or the Jamaica Bay Bridge but instead conceded a change of scenery was welcomed every now and then.

This one Sunday, August 5, 1962, I headed out fishing with some friends to Seagate, which is at the tip of Coney Island. We all had a good day of sun and fun, but not a fish was caught. On the way home, we stopped at Nathan's Famous Restaurant on Surf

Avenue for the best hot dogs on the planet. Nathan's played a local top-forty radio station on loud speakers for all customers to hear while standing and eating on the sidewalk. There was a break in playing music with a news bulletin that Marilyn Monroe was found dead at her Brentwood California home. She was only thirty-six at that time, and her death struck with difficulty to accept. The news reports played over the radio were that she had committed suicide by taking an overdose of barbiturates. I asked myself how such a beautiful woman with all that fame and fortune could commit suicide. The tragedy of her death brought back a memory of when someone in my fifth-grade class brought in a 1956 issue of *Playboy* magazine. My fellow student took it from his father's collection and snuck it into class, and when our teacher stepped away, he opened the centerfold page, and there she was, Marilyn Monroe posing in the nude. It was the first time I ever saw a woman's naked body and recall the beauty of her sitting up with her arms behind her head and the deep-red satin backdrop highlighting her light-pink complexion. Whenever I stop and think about that picture of Marilyn Monroe, my artistic aptitudes take over and view it as a pure work of art.

By 1964, Uncle Curly had purchased a new silver-gray four-door hardtop Pontiac Bonneville, which gave us much more room for all the gear and the additional passengers. The first crabbing trip in my uncle's new car was to Pelican Island, which was about an hour and a half ride from Brooklyn. It was a little difficult spot to crab in because parking was at least a mile away, and dropping off all the gear was a challenge. But Uncle Curly was obsessed with the idea that we could always catch more crabs at the corner spot of the bridge, and getting up at 4:00 a.m. in the morning was a small price to pay. Some of the best times of our lives took place at Pelican Island, and they gave me a strong family tie with my uncle Curly.

Uncle Curly's presence always displayed funny moments while fishing, and one example is the way he positioned his fishing pole between his legs while reeling in his line. Chick and I would always look at each other and smile at his quirky mannerisms. He was also an avid New York Yankee fan who constantly talked about the Yankee teams and players of the past and how they would rate with those present-day players of the early 1960s. At this point in time, I began to look upon my uncle as a father figure in my life while filling the void created from losing one.

> "We do not remember days, we remember moments."
>
> —Cesare Pavese

CHAPTER 3

—I'm on your side. When times get rough.

By the time I was twelve years-old I needed money for clothes and school supplies. I knew that Grandma Rose didn't have any funds to spare, so I decided to earn some money on my own. This is when I found out that no one would hire a twelve year-old anyway. In New York City, a child had to be thirteen years old for employment, and working papers were needed. Chick found a job with Packers Supermarkets, which was only around the corner from home. There was only one small problem, and that was you worked only for tips and were not given any wages. The way it worked was that each store customer paid twenty-five cents per delivery, which went to the driver in charge, who used his own vehicle. That twenty-five cents had to cover the driver's cost of gas and maintenance. So the delivery boys worked for tips only and had to do a good job and convince the customer that the service rendered was worth an extra tip in addition to the twenty-five cents they already paid. Sometimes it was a hard sell, but most people understood and tipped us something anyway. Those who gave nothing had to be given the same courteous service, or the store manager would see to it that the driver had to let you go. It didn't take long before we automatically knew which customers would tip and which ones wouldn't. The driver of the vehicle was named Mike Masterlone, and there were already seven delivery boys including Chick, who persuaded Mike to make room for one more (myself). All of us worked out of his green 1952 Oldsmobile coupe with the backseat ripped out, leaving additional space in the trunk area for boxes of groceries. All eight of us delivery boys had to sit on the fenders of the Oldsmobile and hold on tight so we wouldn't fall off while moving. Sometimes even the police would stop the vehicle, and Mike, who knew most local policemen, talked his way out by explaining that he would drop off all of us around the corner. Mike never dropped us off, and we all then just continued on and paid no attention to what the police wanted. This wasn't the safest workplace environment for an eleven-year-old, but it was a way to make some quick money, and the camaraderie among all us delivery boys lasted for many years.

A few weeks later, Chick and I then figured out a plan for some extra tips from customers, which included the store manager's approval and some real hustling on our part. On Fridays, at about 4:00 p.m., customer orders were shut off for delivery until Saturday morning. Both Chick and I waited until after 6:00 p.m., and then we took boxes of delivery orders home by shopping carts and laid them out in Grandma's backyard. There we staged the boxes by delivery address and reloaded them on the same carts and delivered them that same Friday night instead of Saturday morning. Customers loved the value-added service and tipped us accordingly, and this allowed me to see the benefits of true entrepreneurship for the first time.

In the early years, Chick, Buster, and I shared the rear bedroom with Buster in a foldout bed and Chick and I sharing a twin bed. My sister Gerry slept with Grandma Rose in her twin bed in the next bedroom. There was a chest of drawers in the rear bedroom that stood next to my side of the bed, which was filled with old photos of the family that Chick and I would really enjoy perusing. This was where I saw for the first time what my uncle Joe looked like before

he was killed while serving in the army
photos, my body felt like something wa:
very handsome young man that sported a
like Boston Blackie in the early days of T
presence always showed well in these old p
hard for me to picture him dying in a pla.
the army.

These old photos were a showcase fille(
that I was very eager to learn more about. ...... grandparents' wedding and parent's baby and young-adult photos were just piled up in drawers, not in albums or boxes. Gazing over all those photos, which spanned at least a forty-year period, gave me a sense of reconnecting with my family roots. There also were three large albums filled with newspaper clippings of everything about Joe DiMaggio's baseball career as a New York Yankee, and I found out that my aunt Anna was an avid fan and belonged to his fan club.

Chick and I would try to find photos of relatives who had changed in appearance, and we laughed out loud when a picture would show a relative with more hair and forty pounds lighter than we knew them. There were many photos of relatives at dinner tables or backyard parties and especially during the Great Depression and WWII years. At many sessions, we would find a person in the photo wearing a US Army uniform whom we didn't know, and in the photo, he seemed to be a dear friend with everyone in the photo. So Chick would take the photo and ask Grandma Rose who the person was, but she would just pay no attention to us. We then would bring the photo to Chick's mom, my aunt Dolly. She would give a funny look at first and stare at it for a while without answering the question. Then she would take the photo and walk away, and we would never see that photo again. We even asked my aunt Anna who the person was, but her reply was "Just a family friend whose name I don't recall." The family's reaction to our inquisitive desire to know the person in those photos always remained in both our minds as something very strange, to say the least.

Fun and games on West Tenth Street included the usual sports that city boys played, such as stickball and football, if we were lucky

...ve one available. In many cases, we couldn't afford even ...ball for stickball, so we would have a game called hit the ...ner, which was played using a milk container flattened and ...led up with a rubber band to hold it together and an old broomstick for a bat. The game was played batting opposite: right-handed would bat left-handed and vice versa. Two or four players on each team were positioned across the street. A grounder not caught through the infield was a single, and a fly not caught on the sidewalk was a double. A fly not caught against the opposite house stoop was a triple, and a fly over the stoop was a homerun.

We all also played other games that didn't involve any equipment and had just as much fun as kids could have had. Johnny-on-the-pony was a favorite, which included four or five players on each team with one team having a player standing with his back against a wall and a teammate bent over, grabbing the person standing around the waist, and the next player doing the same with the bent-over player and so on, creating a "pony," and to have the opposing team then run and jump on top of the created phony and try to collapse it to the ground. Ring-a-levio was another game, along with hide-and-seek, tag, and pinching pennies—all fun games that were played without any equipment or cost.

Mushball was a game that needed only a small rubber ball, an old broomstick for a bat, and a wall. A box would be drawn on the wall for the strike zone, and two players, one on each team, could play by pitching the ball into the strike zone and the batter trying

Aunt Dolly with daughters
Donna and Roseann

to hit the ball. The game got its named from the sound of the ball hitting the wall. Four balls and three strikes, just like baseball, were used to advance the game. These games were priceless, and it kept us busy and out of trouble while growing up.

Growing up in the early 1960s involved many major snowstorms that bring back pleasant memories of how hard labor could turn into a fun thing to do. Both my uncles kept a small side business of delivering groceries that my grandfather Filippo operated when he was alive. Because of the business delivery van and the tight driveway and garage situation, no snow could be left on the ground after a snowstorm so the delivery van could make its way out onto the street. So when it snowed, my grandma Rose would fry potatoes and eggs in her trusted, well-seasoned giant black frying pan and serve it on fresh Italian bread sandwiches. The smell would carry throughout the backyard and driveway, and it would attract some certain friends on the block, who would come and help with the snow shoveling.

My grandma Rose's brother Joe worked for the New York City Department of Sanitation, and he made available all the professional-size shovels needed. Some of the shovels were so big it took two of us kids to push it against the snow. We also had a tool that would open the manhole covers in the middle of the street, allowing us to push the snow into the sewer system instead of piling it up. When done, we would be the only house on the block not having a drop of snow anywhere on the concrete, leaving it bone-dry. Our friends knew that after the work was completed, coming in from the bitter cold, there would be a steamy, hot small feast of potato and eggs waiting for them.

My best friend Frank Coppa and I would also go out and shovel snow for local store owners who were willing to pay us for the service. We would charge one dollar per storefront to push the snow into the street since it took only ten or fifteen minutes depending on how much snow fell. The giant sanitation shovels made the job easier, and when the day was over, we did pretty well.

One day, we were working in the neighborhood along Avenue X, and a maid dressed in all white approached us and asked if we would be interested in shoveling snow where she worked and pointed to the house on the corner across the street. The house was the biggest in the area and had a large white iron fence around the property with enormous gates. We both said yes and went over to shovel the sidewalks around the house, the steps, and the driveway. It only took the both of us about a half an hour to finish when we talked about how much to charge and decided that five dollars was a very good price and would settle on three dollars if we really had to. We walked to the opened side door that only had the glass storm door closed, and I rang the bell. A big well-tanned man came to the door, wearing a suit, and peeked out the opened door to look at our work then reached into his front pants pocket and pulled out a large roll of bills larger than I ever saw before. He peeled off a fifty-dollar bill and said, "Would this do it, boys?" and I looked at Frank's expression, and we both just nodded yes since we were speechless. He handed over the money and then asked us if we would always come and shovel the property when it snowed. Both of us again were at a loss for words, and we nodded again and walked away. When we turned the corner, we couldn't believe what just happened. We felt like we won a lottery.

Both of us continued for a few years going to that Avenue X house and gladly shoveled after each snowfall. One snow just before Christmas, we were given a crisp new hundred-dollar bill for the half hour of work. I consider it a leap of faith that this money found its way to us, knowing that there were no two more deserving kids who really needed it. Frank and I had a difficult time trying to cash it. First, we tried local stores, but nobody wanted any part of having us making a small purchase to break a hundred-dollar bill. Then we went to the Lincoln Savings Bank on Avenue X and walked up to a teller, who took the bill and ran to the bank manager. The manager felt the bill, then rubbed it, and then held it to the light, while he gave us both the look of bewilderment. The bank manager asked us where we got the bill, and we explained that the big house just a few blocks away gave it to us for shoveling snow. The bank manager then quickly stepped behind the counter and opened the teller's cash drawer and gave us a small pile of fives and singles in exchange for the hundred-dollar bill. It wasn't until four or five years later that Frank and I found out that the residence belonged to the famous mafia leader named Carlo Gambino, head of the New York crime family, and the big guy who gave us our instructions and payment was his head henchman.

Me & Frank Coppa

My mother would show up every now and then, between boyfriends, and make hell for us at Grandma's house. She would lie on the couch all day/night and, while doing so, only watched CBS channel 2. If we kids wanted to watch our regular shows, she would immediately change the TV back to CBS. She also did it when she was asleep and suddenly woke up. Chick would start arguing, and Mom would all of a sudden say, "You're just like the fuckin' soup." I heard that comment she made many times and couldn't understand what she meant by it. It also bothered me to witness arguments between Mom and Chick. Hearing the both of them go at it was always a sad moment but in a funny way; it made me feel good to hear Chick put her in her place. Mom's arguing didn't just include Chick; it also included Grandma Rose. In fact, my mother constantly showed her short fuse of a temper to most everyone in the family. Thank God Mom's visits were short stays, and I started to really feel the distance between us growing longer by the day. At this point in my young life,

I couldn't wait for her to leave, and as sad as it sounds, I hoped she'd never come back. Mom was never around when there were birthdays or holidays to be celebrated, and her absence for these events gradually wore off in my mind.

Celebrating Christmas with a decorated tree or lights wasn't something Grandma Rose would allow even though we kids would bring up the subject every year. She would always use the same reason for no Christmas tree or decorations, and that was since her husband, our grandfather, died, she was not rejoicing. However, there were some of our neighbors who would decorate for the Christmas holiday season, with one home on the block that went all out and strung Christmas lights covering their entire home. My aunt Anna and uncle Auggie would invite us to their home in Middle Village, Queens, for a Christmas dinner with all the trimmings. Visiting my aunt and uncle was a real treat. I always enjoyed every moment of the day and left with loving memories. Aunt Anna and Uncle Auggie lost their firstborn son named August at the young age of two years old. Their son was born with a cleft lip and palate and was going through a series of corrective surgeries. On his last surgery, which was only for cosmetic reasons, he died while under anesthesia. Cousin August's sudden death took the family by complete surprise, and as a young boy, I remember it was the saddest funeral service I had ever attended. When I stop and think about what life throws at a person, I always think of my aunt Anna losing her husband, Joe, my namesake, after only two weeks of marriage and then her first son in her second marriage at two years old. I always thought of Aunt Anna and Grandma Rose as the closest things to living saints when I was young and still do to this day.

Grandma Rose, Chick, Buster, Gerry, and I would travel by subway to Aunt Anna's house, and Uncle Auggie would drive us at night for the return trip home. We would arrive at the Woodhaven Boulevard train station and call Aunt Anna when we arrived, and Uncle Auggie would pick us up by car and drive us to his home. The first Christmas when we arrived at the Woodhaven train station and tried to call, the pay phone wasn't working, or so we thought. It took Chick and I a dozen tries to realize that pay phones weren't five cents but ten cents a call. There were times when my sister, Gerry, would announce out loud that she smelled a cigar, and within a minute, my uncle Auggie would show up. Uncle Auggie was an avid cigar smoker, and it seemed amazing that Gerry's keen sense of smell picked up the cigar aroma from that distance.

Aunt Anna's house was always fully decorated in lights, and she had a giant fresh-cut Christmas tree lit up in her living room. There were always loads of presents underneath. There would also be nothing but Christmas music playing on a Victrola in addition to a classic Christmas movie on TV, engaging me in a complete holiday spirit. Aunt Anna would make sure she had a gift for each of us under the tree, and it made me feel like we belonged to a normal family for at least that day of the year.

> In every conceivable manner, the family is the link to our past, bridge to our future.
>
> —Alex Haley

CHAPTER 4

—And friends just can't be found.

West Tenth Street was filled with baby boomer kids and their parents whose blue-collar vocations included construction, civil service, and working the docks. Among all those kids, there was one who became a special friend, and his name was Frank Coppa. Frank was an orphan. His mother had died in childbirth, and his father had died on the job a few years later, leaving Frank in the care of his abusive uncle Pete. With Frank being only a year older than me, and neither of us having parents around, we were almost in the same boat and became very close, trying to work out our misfortunes. In 1962, I went to work for a junior high school teacher named Mr. Fisher, and he was partners with another teacher from Borough Park Brooklyn named Mr. Reich. The business was Ocean Breeze Day Camp for children grades four through seven based inside the Washington Baths Pool and Recreation Center complex on West Twenty-First Street and Surf Avenue/the Boardwalk in Coney Island, Brooklyn.

Washington Baths was built in the early 1900s, and it encompassed a square city block filled with outdoor activities such as handball, swimming, diving, tennis, ping-pong, and bocce, all operated for members only. The day camp was a separate business and took advantage of the amenities the pool complex had to offer. I was asked by both owners if I knew someone who was willing to work on weekends and subsequently referred Frank. The job covered construction work on weekends during the spring and fall seasons and five days a week during the summer months. The pay was a flat five dollars per day tax-free and sometimes included long work days prior to the summer season opening. Mr. Fisher found out that I was artistic and had me restore an old mural of cartoon characters painted on a long exterior wall around the side of the day camp. It took me weeks to fill in faded and worn-out areas, but when it was finished, it made the entire grounds look new again.

Frank and I enjoyed the construction work as well as the newfound camaraderie of Mr. Brown. Mr. Brown was a friend of the owners and a retired engineer. He became a mentor to Frank, who absorbed all he could and used his special gift of asking the right questions. At this point in Frank's life, I think he found his calling, because he used this intelligence to eventually become an environmental engineer.

Chick, Frank, and I constantly hung around each other and went fishing together often. One day, Chick and I planned a night fishing trip with Frank, but we knew Grandma Rose would never have let us leave the house at midnight to fish then return at daylight the next morning. So we came up with the idea of setting all the clocks in the house ahead six hours at bedtime and thought Grandma would never know the difference. That next night, our plan went without a ripple, but Grandma kept asking why it was so dark at 6:00 a.m. in the morning. She even started her morning ritual of ironing clothes. Chick and I really had a hard time holding in our laughter but managed to carry out our plan. We left and met up with Frank, whose uncle couldn't care less where he was going. Then we three rode on a bike to Steeplechase Pier in Coney Island for some real night fishing. It turned out that night was a not a good one for catching any fish, and we ended up among some of the weirdest characters life had to offer.

The three of us even witnessed two evil-looking men stuffing newspapers into the crevices around a sleeping homeless man lying on the deck of the pier. The two evil men then took out their Zippo lighters and ignited the newspapers. They both thought it was the funniest thing to do. It took the homeless man about a minute to realize he was on fire when he suddenly woke up screaming and started to roll around, trying to extinguish himself while both men laughed themselves silly. At this point, we had our fill of fishing. We then returned home, but we never got the chance to reset the clocks because Grandma was so mad she started chasing us with her trusty old broom, aiming for both of our shins while having a small smile on her face.

    Another place we fished on Sundays was a concrete supply company named Turacumo Brothers, which was located on the water along the Belt Parkway service road and Bay Parkway in the Bensonhurst section of Brooklyn. The company was closed on Sundays, so Chick, Frank, and I would secretly climb over the barbed wire hurricane fence and walk to the end of the property where the piers were. Each of their piers were massive in size and used for unloading huge barges of sand, stone, and gravel. The complex was filled with dump trucks, cranes, bulldozers, and giant mixing vats that were used in the production of concrete. It was not exactly a safe place for kids to play, but we had a goal in mind, and that was to catch eels.

    For some reason, the only fish caught at this place were eels, and they were big ones, sometimes measuring three feet and over. It is an Italian custom to serve eels on Christmas Eve as part of the Seven Fishes tradition. Catching eels was fun, but landing them in a hemp sack without touching them was almost impossible, since eels are covered in a slimy film. Holding an eel with your bare hands would never work, and they would easily wiggle out and away, leaving their slimy film on your hands and arms. The film wouldn't wash off without a strong detergent and brushing for a very long time, and the smell would get worse as the minutes rolled by. We developed a tool that helped immensely. We dipped a heavy-duty work glove in glue and then, while still wet, dipped it in sand. Then we'd let it dry overnight. The sand-coated glove allowed us to take hold of the eels and place them in sacks to take home. Once we got the eels home, Uncle Curly would drive a large nail through the eel's head into a wood plank, thus holding it firmly in place. With a razor knife, he made a slit just below and around the eel's head. Then he'd put on the special pair of gloves and pull down on the skin, peeling it off the eel. The head would then be removed, leaving nothing but a large strand of white meat with a bone in the center. When the entire process was complete, the eel filets were placed in plastic bags and frozen until needed.

The three of us had our favorite fishing spots that we trekked to by bicycle (three on a bike with gear), depending on what kind of fish were running. Steeplechase Pier in Coney Island, Jedi's at Seagate, and a seawall at Fort Hamilton were all located within Brooklyn. I was always the one who pedaled the bike roundtrip, and it had to be well constructed to carry all the weight. My first bike was purchased for six dollars, and it was a very used and corroded Schwinn that I oiled and sanded for many hours to remove the rust. Uncle Curly had a spraying compressor, and he sprayed it with a few coats of gold-leaf paint that sparkled when sunlight reflected off it. The bike looked fantastic when finished and attracted much attention whenever I rode it. That bike lasted for many years.

The three of us had all worked hard to earn extra money so we could buy good fishing gear, which included Penn fishing reels that we put on layaway plans at Smithy's or Mike's Fishing Tackle stores on Emmons Avenue in the Sheepshead Bay section of Brooklyn. There were times when we biked all the way to Sheepshead Bay just to deposit another fifty cents toward layaway. Nothing seemed to stop us. One time we even braved gale-force winds and an incoming hurricane just to make it to Mike's Fishing Tackle. I remember dodging those fallen trees the size of buildings and flooded streets with rippling, flowing water. We were so determined to reach that tackle shop and had to maneuver many obstacles along the way. But when we arrived, the tackle shop was closed for business due to the storm. Our hearts were broken. The three of us working, playing sports, or fishing together were things that kept us out of trouble and forged relationships that lasted a lifetime.

> "The truth is you don't know what is going to happen tomorrow. Life is a crazy ride, and nothing is guaranteed."
>
> —Eminem

CHAPTER 5

—When you're down and out.

David A. Boody was a former congressman from New York's second district and the last mayor of the city of Brooklyn, New York, just before it became part of New York City in 1898 as a borough. My junior high school was named after David A. Boody (PS 228), and I attended the school from 1960 to 1962. During those three years, I played on the basketball and track team. There was also a program for all students that offered a nighttime open gymnasium (Night-Center) so kids could play and practice sports and keep out of trouble by staying off the streets. Awards were given to students at the end of the school season for their participation in sportsmanship. Many fond memories of fellow students still lay in my mind. The teacher who ran the Night-Center, Mr. Rosiello, was a shop teacher who taught printing-shop skills to boys. He had a rough way with his methods of teaching, but he ruled the classroom, and when he got to know you, he gave whatever special attention that was needed to each and every student. He was the perfect person to run the Night-Center because he ruled with an iron hand and allowed no shenanigans, but he always got to know each and every one of us and helped us any way he could. Mr. Rosiello's rules taught me how to be tough but not boastful and always be respectful to others. My favorite rule of his, "Always put yourself in the other person's shoes," still comes to my mind now over fifty years later. This simple rule played a large part in my young life and still does today. The New York City Board of Education must have noticed something special about him because he was promoted to principal a few years after my leaving Boody.

Me on Boody Track Team

Thursday, October 27, 1960, started as any other day, and after school, a few friends on the block mentioned that it would be fun to walk to Bay Parkway and Eighty-Sixth Street and hang out. When we arrived there, there was a very large crowd gathering with pickets stating all kinds of what seemed like political talk. I didn't pay much attention to what was going on but, I heard a person being introduced to the crowd as our very own Brooklyn Borough president Vito Battista. I stopped and started listening to what he had to say. I then found out what all the hoopla was about. The borough president was introducing Senator John F. Kennedy of Massachusetts, who was running for president of the United States. He was about to say a few words. I don't know what made me do it, but all of a sudden, I decided to get as close as I could. I was about twenty-five feet from the podium when I looked up and noticed a well-tanned young man standing straight up with pride as he started to speak. His words were limited, but each and every person in the audience paid very close attention. He closed his speech mentioning that he knew of a good restaurant in the neighborhood, and the crowd roared out with laughter. I assumed he was talking about a local eatery around the corner named the Famous Cafeteria, where most kids hung out on Friday nights. The future president's words were absorbed by all of us, and we felt his presence for a long time to come because of his references to our neighborhood; he was now one of us.

At school the next day, all we talked about was the presidential race between Richard Nixon and John Kennedy. For the first time in my life, I realized how intricate and important politics were, and I tried to learn everything I could. Witnessing and watching the mannerisms of JFK in person, even though it was a very short time frame, gave me a sense of what my future focus in life should be. My focus would have to change from not being aware to staying fully informed and aware what was going on in the world.

At this time in my life, I began to visit special places in the world through my talent of using art. I was able to place myself mentally into beautiful places that I knew I would never get a chance to visit. I also started to feel and imagine myself in such places as the rocky shores of Monterey, Canada, or the deserts of the Southwestern United States. My favorite artist was Robert Wood, who immigrated to the United States from England. He made his famous claim by roaming the United States from Maine to California in search of landscape subjects.

I began getting interested in art classes that the school had to offer, and in the seventh grade, I had an art teacher named Ms. Neary. She would take a chosen group of us out to local hospitals and shopping districts to paint murals in hallways or storefront windows. When the holidays of Halloween, Thanksgiving, Hanukkah, and Christmas came around, local merchants sponsored awards for best murals in certain categories, and I received many of them. This gave me a special pride for my artistic skill of creating something real that other people could enjoy. By the time I was in the eighth grade, I took a test and applied to New York Art and Design High School in Manhattan and was accepted. Unfortunately, I had to decline due to the cost of travel and supplies that I couldn't afford. It was necessary to work after school, and travelling back and forth to Manhattan five days a week wasn't very practical for me. But my creative rhythm wouldn't sit still, so even though I wasn't going to attend a special art school, I was going to stay fully engaged in art and use my special skills for other people, not just self-enjoyment.

My childhood friendships at Boody were numerous, especially with both my teammates on the basketball and track teams. Nonetheless, there was a classmate named Howie Springer, who was one of the very few African American kids attending Boody. The school was located in a white neighborhood of Italian descent with a public housing project at the fringe of the neighborhood called the Marlboro Projects. I surmise that he lived in that public housing project, but I'm not sure, since he kept his private life to himself. Howie was a big kid that looked much older than everyone else in class and came to school each and every day dressed in a suit, white shirt, and tie, which was never the case with the general student population. He spoke with a very slow and deep voice with ample conviction and was very athletic in gym classes. I would always ask him why he didn't play on the basketball team. He always replied with the same vibrating deep voice, "Nope, can't do that."

It was a typical spring day in April 1961 when the last bell sounded, ending the school day. I was now in the eighth grade, and as I walked out of the school building, I heard a commotion on the side street exit stairs. There were at least twenty-five male students gathered in a circle, chanting "Hit him harder" and "Kick him harder," and as I walked closer, I noticed the school bully beating on someone who wasn't fighting back at all, just bent over, taking the blows of the bully. I pushed my way to the inner circle of the fight and observed Howie Springer being pummeled. Watching a friend being beaten didn't register well in my mind even though one of the school's toughest guys was doing the beating. I debated if I should just walk away from a friend or help stop the fight and face the consequences with the bully and his gang. I decided to jump in and grab the bully around the neck and try to hold him back while yelling out that this has to stop. The bully then tried to turn the fight on me, but I was able to grab both his hands by his fingers and turn my wrist upward, squeezing hard. This maneuver resulted in a lot of pain to him, and to my surprise, none of his friends tried to stop me. I looked at Howie and saw in his eyes that he was much appreciative of my actions. It was a look that would live on and never be forgotten. All the yelling finally stopped, and I let go of the bully. He walked away, not even looking back at me. For the remainder of my years at Boody, that bully never would again try to start anything with Howie or me. Most of my classmates showed considerable respect when they heard what had happened and also felt it was the right thing to do. Howie Springer never showed up at Boody the following year for the ninth grade, and I don't know if he quit school or just moved away. This whole event made me learn that being a good person can pay off in the future, and you never know when a good deed will be repaid.

During my Boody years, I worked for another supermarket that had the same delivery boy situation as when I was eleven years old, but this store only had two of us as helpers. The driver was named Vinnie Gallo, and the other helper was named Gaspar Giordano. I didn't have much respect for the driver, Vinnie, who, by the way, had a bad stuttering problem. He was married with two kids who lived in total despair. Whenever I saw his wife, who was stunningly beautiful, try to manage the family without Vinnie's help, it made me sick to my stomach. At that time, Vinnie dated a girl in my ninth grade class who was at least fifteen years younger than him, and he would take her out and spend the needed money while depriving his own family. His children needed braces and eyeglasses, but it didn't seem to matter. When Vinnie would stop home while working, I would recall during those visits my father and his cheating on our family. Even though I was only fourteen years old, I knew the outcome wouldn't be a good one for Vinnie, his wife, or their small children. Even though I was far from having my own family, instinctively I knew how important it was to not make the same mistakes made by both my parents.

During this time frame, my mother finally divorced my father and remarried. Her new husband's name was Joe Morris. Joe was a Boston College alumni and former merchant marine turned bartender. He worked in a large bar on the corner of West Twenty-Third

Street and Ninth Avenue in Manhattan called Smithy's. Mom and Joe rented an apartment on the corner of Grandma Rose's block, and she immediately started to try and confuse me and my siblings with new problems. Her new husband, Joe, was a drunk and would, on his days off, arrive in the early mornings, toting a case of Rheingold Beer and two-fifths of J&B scotch. He sat at the kitchen table, drinking and making me sit with him to listen to how life didn't treat him well by giving him the short end of the stick. His knowledge was amazing because of his Boston College education, and ironically he was probably was one of the smartest people I had ever met. But he wasted it all on alcoholism. Chick and I nicknamed him the Bureaucrat, because of his keen knowledge on politics.

In 1962, Mom purchased a brand-new white Chevy II Super Sport convertible with bucket seats, a black top, and red interior, and she told me that in three years, when I turned eighteen, she would give me the Chevy II on my high school graduation. Telling me that the car would be mine someday gave me something to look forward to, but it also helped make Joe's drinking a little more pliable. Every chance I had to be involved cleaning and waxing that car, I'd take it. I'd even sneak and take it for a spin around the block without a driver's license. Sitting behind the wheel, driving that Chevy II as a fifteen-year-old, gave me a feeling of independence as I daydreamed of someday being able to go wherever I wanted whenever I wanted.

One late morning, the front doorbell rang at Grandma Rose's, which was not a normal thing to happen since we only used the rear entrance. It was the police, who had Joe Morris in tow, completely drunk, and I'll never forget him saying, "One day you don't read the paper and they build a monument in front of you." He wasn't hurt in any way, which is still hard to believe even today. The police explained that Joe was driving and smashed into the Grand Army Plaza entrance for Prospect Park in Brooklyn. The plaza was built in 1867 and honored those Union soldiers whose lives were lost in the Civil War. It's a massive structure, 131 feet high and about 100 yards wide, that could never be missed when driving by it, and there was Joe Morris saying that stupid drunken quote about not reading the newspaper and building a monument in front of him.

When I think back now, I don't know why he wasn't arrested and charged with drunken driving, but I guess in those days, the police had other priorities. Once the police were leaving, one of the officers said, "Oh, by the way, that white convertible is a total wreck. It was towed to a junkyard nearby." My heart sank like a rock, and I almost came to tears right then. I couldn't believe that my dream of independence was now over or that it was sunk by nothing less than a simple drunk. My mother always made things worse just by being around. She would begin quarreling with Grandma over what seemed nothing. Likewise, she and Chick were like oil and vinegar, and when they were in the same room, it wouldn't take long before they'd go at it. The comment about Chick being "just like the fuckin' soup" always came up to end the conversation, but I never understood what she meant.

Roughly two or three weeks later, Joe Morris showed up at Grandma Rose's on a dreary rainy day at about 8:00 a.m. in the morning with his typical liquor stash and started drinking away. Within a few hours, he started getting very belligerent with me, and I didn't want to be near him any longer. The sight of him disgusted me. I left the kitchen, and he muttered something out loud, which I dismissed by putting on my jacket and heading outside for some fresh air. He followed me, yelling "You little bastard," and caught up with me on the front porch. He then started to climb the brick steps, and when he just about reached the top, I thought about what he would do to me when he got his hands on me. I quickly saw an opportunity, so I let loose with a right-hand punch to the left side of his face, and he suddenly stopped in his tracks. Then he fell backward down the steps, bouncing along the way down. It was now raining harder. I didn't look back. I just ran inside and told Grandma what had happened. We both went upstairs and peered out of the front window, seeing Joe Morris lying facedown on the brick steps in the rain.

I stayed sitting at that front window for what seemed a few hours. He moved a leg or arm every now and then but was so drunk he didn't feel anything. Finally, he did get up and started walking back toward his apartment on the corner. Grandma called my mother and told her what had happened and that she didn't want him in her house again. Apparently, Joe Morris probably didn't treat Mom any better, and she shortly filed for divorce, and I never saw him again, which was fine with me. Mom also moved out of her apartment on the corner to an unknown place and left our lives once again. But there wasn't any sadness left in my heart this time. I was actually happy to see her go.

"Life is not a problem to be solved, but
a reality to be experienced."

—Soren Kierkegaard

CHAPTER 6

—When you're on the street.

Living without any child support from either my mom or dad now became a serious problem for Grandma Rose, since we kids needed food, clothes, and medical/dental care, along with other normal items kids our age needed. My uncle Sal and Aunt Cathy tried to help and had asked a neighborhood lawyer what we could do. The lawyer gave them free advice, so it was determined that Grandma Rose and I would go to the domestic relations court in downtown Brooklyn and seek counsel from a judge. It was an hour's travel time on the subway including the walk from the station to the courthouse. This was one of the hardest times of my life, and we both sat for hours, waiting to be interviewed and met with the judge. My grandmother's name was finally called by the court bailiff, but I would be the one to do all the talking since my grandmother spoke broken English and wasn't a verbal communicator. I knew how important this was, so I tried my best for a thirteen-year-old, and it apparently worked as the judge seemed very attentive to our problem. She spoke to me as an adult with respect, then called for a recess and asked Grandma Rose and me to follow her into her chambers.

Once in the judge's chambers, she explained to us that she was issuing a warrant to arrest my father for lack of child support. The warrant was going to be in my name as server, and it would give me the authority to present it to any policeman to arrest my father. The judge also gave me her card with a special phone number that any arresting officer could call for verification. It was also explained to me that finding my father's location by the court would take some time and that I had a better chance of finding him since I already knew his general whereabouts. My grandmother's brother's son who worked for Eastern Airlines on Third Avenue and East Fiftieth in Manhattan would see my father often at lunchtime, walking around the area of his office building.

It certainly was a good place to start my search, so I started taking a day at a time off from school and walked around that area, looking for my dad. On the second day of searching the neighborhood without really noticing where I was, I suddenly found myself again at the foot of the Fifty-Ninth Street Bridge. The stores across the street from the bridge on Second Avenue were still antique shops filled with the same type of furnishings as my dad's store had been filled with just a few years before. Nothing seemed to have changed much, even the coffee shop on the corner was still there, reminding me of the many times my dad asked me to run out and purchase him coffee. I recalled special moments when Dad gave me an extra fifteen cents to buy myself a pineapple Popsicle, and the coffee shop owner would say, "Watch out, kid. It might blow up," referring to pineapples and what German hand grenades were called in WWII.

It was still late morning, so I decided to walk over the Fifty-Ninth Street Bridge and try to locate the spot where my brother and I were dropped off by my mother. Following the pedestrian walkway, it took me out and over the raging East River water below. I stopped where I thought the spot was, but after deep thought, I came to the conclusion that my brother and I were left on what looked like a catwalk that had access from the roadway since the pedestrian walkway had no access to the roadway. It all started to feel kind of fuzzy, but the location was spot-on. I looked up and noticed pigeon nests squeezed between the iron girders of the bridge, giving them total protection from the weather. There were pigeon droppings everywhere, so thick a shovel would be needed to remove them. Since it was daylight this time, looking downriver, I recalled the same passing of tugboats and barges with the sounds of fog horns in the distance. The flow of traffic was now vibrant and noisy and nothing like I remembered that wicked night. Whenever I heard a car horn, it took me back to that night, wishing and hoping it was my father coming to the rescue in his green step van. I also began to recall the promise I made to God that if he answered my request, I would never ask for help again. The wind twisting through and bouncing around those steel beams then seemed to encircle me. Pigeon feathers that were lying near me started to swirl around me while giving me some sort of sign that all was well now. At that moment, I knew that I could come up with the strength to follow through with my mission.

It took the third day when I noticed my father walking out of a convenience store, and I followed him to an antique bookshop on Second Avenue and Fifty-First Street. The store was a few steps below the street level, and it appeared to me that he owned and operated the business. It was a Friday, and now I had a place where I could have the warrant served, so I planned on returning the following Monday.

During that weekend, all I thought about was how I was going to get this accomplished and shivered just thinking about it. I had trouble sleeping the next two days and said to myself, "This is my father I'm going to have arrested. Will I be able stand up and do it because I knew it was so important? That we needed monetary support for survival?" Those thoughts should not have been coming from a fourteen-year-old, but I needed to gain the strength to just do what had to be done.

That next Monday was another day in my life that will never be forgotten as long as I live. I left home at about 10:00 a.m. and took the subway into midtown Manhattan. During the ride, I couldn't help but think that something was going to go wrong and somehow I would pay the price. I arrived at the Fifty-First Lexington Avenue line station at about 11:00 a.m. and walked a short distance to

Second Avenue and First-First, where I staged myself across the street to watch over that antique bookstore. I kept thinking of how close I was to where my dad's original shop was, and wouldn't you know, it started to rain real hard just like that night in 1958. About a half an hour had passed, and out of the corner of my eye, I could see my dad walking on Fifty-First, heading for the store. I waited for him to get settled inside and started looking for a cop. I walked about a block down on Second Avenue and spotted a cop in black rain gear giving out a traffic ticket to a double-parked car. I let the officer finish what he was doing and walked over and said, "Officer, I need your help to serve a warrant for my father's arrest," and motioned to hand him the warrant. The cop was in no mood for doing anything and said, "Get lost, kid," and started to walk away. I couldn't let that happen, and as he was walking, I stepped in front of him. Once again I asked him to help and serve the warrant. This time the officer walked toward me as though he was going to take the warrant, but instead, he grabbed me by the collar of my coat and said, "I warned you, kid. Now I'm going to take you into the station." He then proceeded to drag me for about a block and half and wouldn't let me go until we reached inside the police station. I was taken to the front desk, which was perched up high, and there was a sergeant sitting, shuffling papers, who looked up and said, "What's up with this kid?" Then the street cop told his side of a story that didn't match what really happened.

I was asked by the sergeant, "And what do you have to say about this, kid?" I once again explained what I needed and handed over the warrant to him for his scrutiny. He said that it looked official enough and asked how in the world a court would have a kid serve a warrant on his father. I then also handed him the card that the judge gave me and asked him to call her. The sergeant looked at me over his glasses and stated that this better be for real or else I would be in big trouble. He then reached over to the rotary phone on his desk and dialed the number, and about five seconds later, I could sense someone on the other end picked up.

The sergeant introduced himself and the purpose of his call. Then he got real silent and kept saying, "Yes, Your Honor. Yes, Your Honor. I will, Your Honor," and hung up. The receiver was placed back on the phone, and he then told the street officer to go with me and arrest whoever I pointed out and bring them into the station for booking.

The street cop was now in a worse mood and kept mumbling, "Why me? Why me?" as we both walked back down to Second Avenue, where we reached the front of the antique bookstore. I noticed my dad walking about with a tray of books in his arms, and as I started to go down the few steps into the doorway, he happened to look out and noticed me with the cop close behind me. I opened the door, and Dad walked toward me, saying, "Joe, what are you doing here?" With a squeaky voice, I replied, "I'm having you arrested. Grandma can't support us any longer." At this point, my father's face turned very pale, and the expression was filled with both surprise and anger. The street cop reached for the back of his belt and flipped a set of handcuffs out and asked my father to turn around with his hands behind and cuffed him. Dad told the cop that his keys to lock the store were in his jacket pocket, and I reached in and got the keys and locked the door. Then the three of us walked around the block back to the police station.

When we arrived at the station, the sergeant noticed us right away and motioned us to walk up to the desk. He explained to my dad that he was going to be booked, and he had already made arrangements for a paddy wagon to transport him to the court in Brooklyn. I would be also taken in a separate police car. I then found out that my dad was using two different names instead of his real name. Phil Colby and Phil Fontana were his aliases. The desk sergeant told me that he apparently used the names regularly and had IDs to show it. My dad was taken to a holding cell, and I was taken to what looked like a break room that had a table and chairs, a coffeepot, and a refrigerator. The street cop stayed with me and started to open up a little, apologizing to me for being rough on me. He asked me some questions about who was taking care of us and where my mother was in all this. I answered all his questions and briefly explained the circumstances. Then he looked puzzled and said he didn't understand how parents could do what my own had done and handed me a Pepsi. Within about forty-five minutes, the paddy wagon arrived, and I was taken by police car with sirens blasting, following all the way downtown and over the Brooklyn Bridge to Flatbush Avenue and on to the courthouse.

Once at the courthouse, I was taken to a waiting room that was wood paneled, resembling a courtroom, and handed over to a bailiff. The street cop then wished me good luck and saluted as he turned and walked away. I sat there for a short time as nervous as can be, and then another bailiff came into the room and motioned me to walk through a doorway that went directly into a courtroom, and I was seated in the first row. This was the first time I ever stepped foot inside a real courtroom. All I could think of were those TV episodes of *Perry Mason*. There were a few other people in the courtroom, and everyone was very quiet. One of the bailiffs asked us to rise. I don't remember the presiding judge's name, but he was not the same judge that was handling my case. Another door on the opposite side of the courtroom opened, and out came my father with a bailiff at his side, and he stood in front of the judge. The judge shuffled through some papers and started to question my father, asking why he hadn't supported his children. My father explained that things were rough and he sent whatever he could. He said he also just happened to have a check with him and handed it over to the bailiff. The judge never asked for me to confirm a word my father said. He just looked at my father, stated that he looked like an honorable man, and indicated that he was going to take his word. He then added that if my dad ever showed up in his courtroom again, he would throw the book at him. I knew what that meant, and I couldn't believe what was happening right in front of my eyes. The check was only for two hundred dollars, but it was handed over to me. Then the judge dismissed the courtroom. Apparently, Dad had a check with him and was able fill it out while in custody. My father was taken out the same door he'd entered. Then I walked, left the courthouse, and took the subway home, thinking how wrong the whole situation had been, and knew that we weren't going to see any other checks in the future.

No surprise to me, the next month came and went, and month after month no check arrived. It was decided that I return to court and start the whole process over again, which I did, and had my father arrested for a second time about eight months later. I went through the entire procedure once again, but this time with different characters but the same story plot and final curtain. In those years, courts were not aggressively attacking deadbeat dads, though over time, as reported in the media, things have changed for the better.

During these tough times of trying to find my father and going through the court system, going to school got pushed to the backseat in my life. Occasionally, I just had to do something different and break out of a deep rut I was in and get my mind to thinking a healthier thought. So one day, during my eighth-grade year when Boody was offering special noontime dancing at the lunch period, a classmate of mine suggested we go to noontime dancing and see what it was all about. The chaperone was a teacher named Mrs. Tolins, who was an old battle-ax who happen to be the wife of the dean of boys, Mr. Tolins. All the girls would eat quickly and go to the girl's gym for dancing. Hardly any boys ever showed up. It sounded like a different thing to do, so I agreed. When we entered the girl's gym, music was playing from a 45 rpm Victrola, which sounded like a familiar scratchy noise. As I walked to the other side of the gym, it seemed that a few boys gathered on the opposite side of the girls, and all the dancing was between girls only. Mrs. Tolins stood in the center of the gym with a ruler in her hand that she slapped against the side of one leg. I looked across the gym and noticed a girl that I had a crush on named Lorraine Bitetto standing with a girlfriend and giving me a strange look like "What is he doing here?" The fourth or fifth song played was "The Peppermint Twist" by Joey Dee and the Starliters. I was never any good at dancing, but I knew the twist was easy, so I walked across and asked Lorraine to dance. She accepted. As soon as we started to dance the twist, everyone in the gym circled around us and watched while clapping their hands with joy. When the dance was over and the music stopped, Mrs. Tolins started yelling that the twist was not allowed since it was "the dance of the devil." Her rules were broken, and Lorraine and I were to follow her and report to her husband's office for disciplinary actions. It was all so quick I couldn't believe what just had happened. One minute I finally got my mind off my difficulties and the next I ended up with a new problem.

Lorraine and I followed Mrs. Tolins to Mr. Tolins's office, and once we entered, she started raising her voice in front of Mr. Tolins. She gave him a mouth of rubbish about us breaking her rules at noontime dancing. Mrs. Tolins demanded that she wanted to see both our parents the next day and took Lorraine with her to another office for further disciplinary actions and left me with her husband. Mr. Tolins was a no-nonsense dean of boys who had a dead pinky on his right hand that would hang when he pledged allegiance to the flag. This finger was also used by him to slap the heads of those troublemakers who crossed his path, and it felt like a rock when you were hit. He asked me why I broke the rules in noontime dancing. I replied I didn't know about the rule and also asked how dancing the twist could be against the rules if it was being played. He then had a look on his face of confusion and stepped closer to me and slapped the top of my head with that dead pinky. He then told me I was a wise guy and both my parents better be there tomorrow morning to meet with his wife. Then he ordered me to return to my regular class.

After school that day, I mentioned it to Chick, and he told me to take a picture of my mother to Mrs. Tolins, since she wanted to see her and said he used that ploy once with Mrs. Ganito, who was another battle-ax teacher at Boody, who, on your first offense, would have you sit under her desk for disciplinary action and on the second offense would take you home with her and expected you to clean her kitchen floor on your hands and knees. She took me home once to clean the kitchen floor, and I think she really enjoyed this punishment as a way to make her point.

I thought about Chick's advice, but it seemed a little beyond Mrs. Tolins's understanding of my family situation, and she would just think I was being another wise guy. My grandma Rose heard us talking about Mrs. Tolins's demands and unannounced she went to my aunt Dolly, who went to school the next morning to see Mrs. Tolins and apparently explained to her my family situation. While in class the next day, I was called down to Mr. Tolins's office, and when I arrived, he was there with his wife. They both had a totally changed understanding of me and who I was. Mrs. Tolins told me that from that day on, I was entitled to free lunch, and all I had to do was tell the cashier "Number 16." Mr. Tolins walked closer to me, and I trembled, expecting a pinky blow on the head. Instead he placed his arm around me and started to walk with me. He told me if I ever needed to talk about anything, he was there for me. I don't know what my aunt Dolly said or did with Mrs. Tolins, but it must have been a glimpse of what was going on in my life, and I will always remember what my aunt Dolly did for me.

> Success is how high you bounce when you hit bottom.
>
> —George S. Patton

CHAPTER 7

—When evening falls so hard.

How would he react since I had him arrested? Is she a girlfriend? Why is he bringing her here? How young is she?

Two of the only five visits my father ever provided to me and my siblings while living with Grandma Rose were short stays including an accidental run-in while fishing along the Belt Parkway one summer day. This visit was different. I was upstairs, completing an oil pastel seascape, when I happened to look out the front window and notice my dad parking a car across the street. He got out and walked toward Grandma's house. There was another person walking with him, and it was a different slim young female and certainly not Joanne Kelly. I stayed upstairs until Grandma called out from downstairs to come to the kitchen. I really started to think what was in store for me once I faced my father and this person. My heartbeat started to speed up, and I started to feel a tremble in my hands as I dropped a pastel on the floor.

My knees began knocking as I hesitantly made my way down the stairs and walked into the kitchen. There I saw my grandma standing next to my father and the young-looking woman who didn't look much older than me. My face must have been as pale as a ghost as I expected the worst. It came to me that looking my father straight into his eyes would be the best thing to do while also showing no fear. Instead I was introduced to her, and my dad went on to say her name was Pat and that they were recently married in Delaware. I was shocked. It came as a big surprise that dad would get married again, especially to such a young woman as that.

There was a twenty-year difference between their ages, and not to help the situation, Pat looked younger than her age. We all sat at the kitchen table, and Grandma put some coffee and Nabisco social tea wafers on the table, and we started to talk with Pat. We didn't say much, but when she did speak, my grandma couldn't understand her, and she kept asking me where she was from. It was very funny to watch since Pat couldn't understand Grandma's broken English accent either. At this point, nothing was mentioned about me having Dad arrested twice. I certainly wasn't in a position to bring it up since the subject was on a higher level. Throughout the years, my dad never once brought up the arresting incidents, and neither did I. As more time passed, later in life, it all seemed that time just washed away those depraved memories.

Pat was a brunette, about five feet four inches tall and 115 pounds, and in the few words she spoke, I noticed a Southern drawl. She then explained that she was from Tennessee and had been living in Manhattan, working as a hairdresser. I couldn't help but keep staring at her from the corner of my eye, and I'm sure she must have felt very uncomfortable just being there. My dad filled me in on my other grandparents, aunts, uncles, and cousins who were scattered over the Bronx and Long Island. The visit wasn't very long, and Dad said he had to meet friends on Long Island and that they were already late. When they left, my aunt Dolly came running downstairs, asking Grandma and me all kinds of questions about who the woman was and what Dad had to say and if he gave any support money.

The visit ran through my thoughts for a long time, and I would get depressed just thinking of it, with no mention whatsoever of child support for us kids. It's not every day that a sixteen-year-old unexpectedly meets his father's new wife. There was a voice inside, asking, "Why me? Why now?" and somewhere somehow I had to release the confusion going from side to side in my mind. I then began to wonder what life would have been like if we were all together as one big, happy, normal family again. I missed having a mom and dad who would nourish and care for me while growing up, but I understood that was never going to happen. I later came to accept Pat as Dad's wife and my stepmother while also being the best thing he had ever done in his life. Pat ended up a caring and loving person who always tried to repair my relationship with my father. I loved her for it.

Step Mom Pat & Kelly

As my own life was unstable in troubled water, so was the country I loved. I recall a day that I will never forget. It was November 22, 1963. I was a sophomore at Lafayette High School. Over the public address system, all students were called to their homeroom class where we listened to the principal announce that President Kennedy had been shot in Dallas, Texas. Our teacher was crying when she asked that we all bow our heads and say a prayer for his recovery. The principal came on again and announced that all classes were cancelled and we were dismissed to go home. As the classroom started to empty, I walked over to the window on the top floor facing the Verrazano-Narrows body of water and the almost complete construction of the Verrazano-Narrows Bridge and wondered how something like this could ever happen to such a vibrant man that was loved by everyone. It sure was an eerie feeling looking out at a great engineering marvel that touched Brooklyn, just like President Kennedy's visit touched all those people that night in 1960, and that moment hasn't left me. Recalling his presence on stage just a few years before and standing no more than twenty feet away from him with that look of prominence in his eyes still remained in my mind.

When I finally arrived home, I listened to the TV news shows. I recall CBS news anchor Walter Cronkite announcing that the president was pronounced dead at Parkland Hospital. The tears could not be held back, and he removed the black-rimmed eyeglasses to wipe the tears away, trying to comprehend what he had just said. That moment in time seemed as though it was surreal, and it still lingers in my mind.

As a mental release to my family situation, I continued to pursue my athletic abilities in track and field in my sophomore year. My running capabilities were slowed down because I was now lifting weights on a regular basis. Chick then talked me into using my strength by joining the track team as a shot-putter. Chick and Frank were already on the track team, and Chick explained to the coach, Paul Friedman, that I had been practicing over that past summer and looked forward to being on the team. I was the only sophomore shot-putter at that time, and the three seniors treated me lukewarm during our first practice. On the second practice day, I was finally able to put the shot weighing twelve pounds at about forty feet, which was already better than two of the three seniors, except Mike who was at about forty-four feet. When we were lifting weights, I already was by far the strongest of all at the standing military press and bench press lifts. Two of the seniors started to recognize that I had potential, but Mike started to rarely speak to me. I wasn't entered in any competitive meets until the next spring, which was the Novice Champs of New York City held at Randall's Island. Randall's Island is situated in the middle of the East River, or Troubled Water, between Manhattan, the Bronx, and Queens. Once again, those very same troubled waters would have an impact on my life.

The stadium had been a WPA project during the Great Depression years and built for the USA Olympic trials, which included the most famous track sprinter of all time named Jesse Owens. Over the years, the stadium had many other names, being Triborough Stadium, Downing Stadium, and now called Icahn Stadium.

I checked in on arrival with the officials for the shot put event and found out that my coach didn't correctly remember my name at entry, and I was entered as Pete Ruzzudo instead of my real name.

It was a big disappointment for me, and the coach explained it was a mistake and it was too late to make a change, so I would have to compete as Pete Ruzzudo or not compete at all. I wondered to myself what I could do to have my coach remember my name so this would never happen again. I also knew that I was only a short distance from the Fifty-Ninth Street Bridge. Just maybe it could again give me that special strength. By winning this event, it would make my coach remember my real name even though the competition was the entire New York City public school system.

Prior to my second throw, I looked out over the field to where the best throw of the day had been marked. I recognized the fact that something drew me to this place, and I just had to win. That voice became loud and clear once again. "Do this and you will be a survivor." I crossed the eight-foot circle as fast as I could, and the steel metal ball seemed to just roll off my fingers. I could feel the power behind the throw. It had plenty of height and landed about four feet beyond the best throw, and all onlookers started to ooh and aah with applause. The field judge had to run farther out since he wasn't expecting a throw that distance and marked the spot with the measuring tape. It was called out by the circle judge as forty-seven feet and two and three-fourth inches.

Somehow I didn't feel surprised by the distance since my mind was previously made up that I was going to win with a great throw. As it turned out, when my coach came over to me with a great, big smile on his face, he explained to me that not only did I set a school record for any age shot-putter, but I also set a New York City Novice Champ record. The entire track team including Chick and Frank was elated and showed their appreciation. However, Mike the senior shot-putter, quit the team just about a week later. I would return to that very same meet over the next two years. I would open the meet program and turn to the section featuring the shot put competition and read the record holder as Pete Ruzzudo, Lafayette High School. It all still hurts to know that no one but a few teammates knew who the record holder really was. But I didn't let it get me down because there were more important letdowns in my life that had already occurred.

That same sophomore year, I went on to place second in the Brooklyn Champs competition while winning all dual meets Lafayette had between other area high schools. My best throw for that year and another school record was at fifty feet and three-fourth inches during a dual meet with Sheepshead Bay High School. Chick, Frank, and I loved to go to all the 1963 indoor season meets held in the 168th Street Engineers Armory in upper Manhattan next to Columbia Presbyterian Hospital whether we were competitors or spectators. The camaraderie between our teammates and neighboring high schools seated around us leaves many countless memories that still live with me. One of those memories was eating the meatball sandwiches Grandma Rose made for lunches. They had such a fantastic aroma that it travelled to all levels of the armory and turned heads when we started to eat. Everyone around us wished they had those sandwiches, but Chick and I knew they were not just any meatballs; they were also made from love.

In my junior year, I was starting to feel steady pain in my right elbow caused by the forced pushing and snapping of the elbow with a twelve-pound steel ball hundreds of times a week in practice. I also became very ill with serious bronchitis, which almost led to pneumonia. Since I had a 102-degree fever prior to the Brooklyn Indoor Champs, I told my coach that I couldn't compete, but he didn't want to accept that. He promised me that he would drive me to the meet in downtown Brooklyn instead of taking the subway and back home if I also would make an effort for just one throw. I accepted the coach's offer and gave it three tries; however, my strength just wasn't in me that night, and I didn't even make the final round. That's when the coach told me he had to go and wouldn't be able to drive me home. Taking the subway in frigid temperatures was my only other option. There is no question in my mind that travelling home sicker that night and being ill to begin with only aided to a more serious condition. It turned out that I was out of school for about two months and lost a total of fifty pounds. What was left of my junior year was now gone.

My senior year as a shot-putter was a little better but not by much, and my best throw was only fifty-two feet two inches. In the

Brooklyn Champs outdoor season where I again placed second, competing seemed lonely since both Frank and Chick had graduated. My heart was no longer in it. I also had another interest, and that was what a future career was going to be since I wasn't going to college and my education years were coming to an end.

Thanks to teammate and friend Jack Chisomalis, in 1964 I worked at a fast-food place called the Eat-a-Way. It was located within the Stillwell Avenue subway station in Coney Island, Brooklyn. All subway trains ended and led to Coney Island, and it was considered the crossroads of New York City. The big attraction was the beach/boardwalk and Nathan's Famous across the street on Surf Avenue, which drew larger-than-life crowds, but the Eat-a-Way was the first food place customers saw when departing their train. The owners were Big Tony the Greek, who weighed over five hundred pounds and his wife, Mary. This was the first job I had that paid the minimum wage of $1.00 an hour until about November when it jumped to $1.15 an hour. In addition to the Eat-a-Way, they also owned a hot peanut/popcorn stand and an Italian ice stand that were also operated in the train station. I was able to work long hours and brought home a fairly good salary for my age at that time. A good thing Big Tony did was drive me home at night so I didn't have to deal with all the weirdoes in Coney Island. There was a bar across the street named the Pleasant Bar, and the *L* had fallen off the sign, so it was nicknamed the Peasant Bar. The doors to this bar were massive. Frequently fights would start inside the building, and the police would head in riding on horseback to bust up the fights. It was a place that you had to wipe your feet off when you left!

At the Eat-a-Way during the holidays of July 4 and Labor Day, working weekends for twenty-four hours straight wasn't uncommon, and it was so busy the food was being served so fast it didn't have enough time to properly cook. I'll never forget customers walking off the trains demanding their corn on the cob, french fries, hot dogs, or hamburgers and wanting them immediately and choosing not to wait for them to fully cook. No one would ever complain, and partially cooked fast food was eaten and enjoyed by the crowds, especially late at night when it seemed the drunks ruled the streets.

During my senior year at Lafayette, I started having a problem with my English teacher named Mr. Mauna, who was always dressed in a suit and tie and had a military-style haircut. He insisted all boys in his class wear at least a white dress shirt and tie. The school itself didn't have such a rule, and I felt that I wouldn't wear any tie just to his class. Each time, Mr. Mauna would reprimand me in class and sometimes send me to the dean's office. The dean offered to give me a tie and hold it in his office so I could pick it up just before English class. I asked the dean why Mr. Mauna had the power to set dress code that the school didn't have. The dean had no answer for me and sort of smiled with a smirk.

The finals came, which were called the Regents, and I needed to pass with a 65 percent to achieve a commercial course diploma. The day after the Regents, I reported to Mr. Mauna's class to find out my score, and he noticed me and, with a great, big smile, said, "Looks like you failed by only one point," and handed me my mark at 64. This meant that either I couldn't work because I had go to summer school and achieve at least a 65 percent or accept the failure and graduate with a general course. Mr. Mauna won the shirt-and-tie game, and I did graduate with only a general diploma, figuring it didn't matter in my new full-time job search.

Twelve years later, my godson and cousin Chick's brother Joe had Mr. Mauna as an English teacher, who by then had completely turned hippie, with long hair and tie-dyed clothes and no dress rules to follow. Looking back now, I think it was still a victory for Mr. Mauna since he got his way, but not a total loss for me because I sensed his persona as nothing but being a deceptive teacher.

Having some extra money in my pocket for the first time allowed me to start dating a girl in my business law class named Judy Cupo, who was my first steady girlfriend. We began enjoying the spring and summer of 1965 by going to the beach many times and watching movies in theaters and hanging out with friends on Eighty-Sixth Street in Bensonhurst, Brooklyn. Her father was Fred Cupo, and he was the kind of guy you wouldn't want to mess with. He was a motorcycle cop on the Belt Parkway, which ran between Brooklyn and Queens, and he probably ran across some tough individuals in his daily life. On the day of high school graduation, he invited me to dinner and a show with his family at a live performance in Jones Beach Marine Theater on Long Island. The show was South Pacific, and the performers and singers were top-notch Broadway stars of the day. This was the first time I had ever watched a live professional performance. Fred had just taken possession of a brand-new metallic-green four-door 1965 Chevy Impala, and this was his first drive outside the neighborhood. He drove that Chevy with all the pride and glory he had and kept asking me what I thought of the ride. When we arrived at the parking lot of Jones Beach, which was built to accommodate thousands of vehicles, Fred decided to park far away from the crowd because his Chevy would be safer even though it meant a long walk for us to the theater, but everyone seemed in agreement. We all got out of the Chevy and started to walk toward the theater when we heard a squashing sound, and we all looked back and saw another car swipe the side of Fred's new Chevy. It was enough to set Fred off in anger, and we watched him run to the driver of the other car and pull him right out of the vehicle through the opened window. At this point, Judy's mom ran yelling to let the man go, but Fred threw him on the hood of the other car and was about to pop him but held back. Fred began to calm down a little with his wife pulling him away. The other driver quickly handed over his paperwork and said his insurance would pay for the damages. The mood for the rest of the evening was on edge after that, and I didn't know what to say but did recall times when my own father pulled other drivers out through open windows, and I totally understood Fred's rational thinking.

They all finished exchanging documents, and then we headed to the restaurant next to the theater for dinner. Having dinner was enjoyable, and Fred started to open up and the pressure was then released, especially when his wife began joking about the terrified look on the driver's face when Fred pulled out his badge. It was the first time in my life that I ate at a sit-down restaurant and drank my first beer, since I was by then of legal age, having turned eighteen years old a few days prior. The romance with Judy only lasted till about September 1965, when we decided to just remain friends and pursue other interests.

    I had always thought turning eighteen would be my foundation for independence. I also knew that being eighteen years old would allow me to ignore those many threats from my mother. Mom every now and then would yell out loud that she was going to take us kids from Grandma Rose. My response was now, "I'm eighteen and don't want to. We're staying right here with Grandma." Mom never understood the loving bond we kids had with Grandma Rose, and neither did she recognize her lack of showing any thanks to those who helped raise her children. Speaking for myself and my siblings, we were finally in a stable environment with Grandma Rose, and we were not about to change a thing.

"In the end, it's not the years in your life that count. It's the life in your years."

—Abraham Lincoln

CHAPTER 8

—When darkness comes.

I'm not doing that assignment. Who does he think he is? No way am I traveling to Manhattan three times a week after school!

A person might remember a teacher or two after high school for many years, but some students come across a special teacher who becomes part of their everyday lives as they grow older. Being a student who was misplaced and uninterested in learning, I had such a teacher whose name was Mr. Frankel. He was my homeroom and merchandising teacher for two years while in high school. My direction was unknown as a senior, and I was not going to college. My studies were on a commercial course, which included merchandising, bookkeeping, business law, and typing. These studies were meant to directly prepare me for the working world upon graduation. The school chose not to have academic courses available to me since I could not afford college and needed to work as soon as possible after graduation.

One late Friday afternoon, just before dismissing the class for the weekend, Mr. Frankel gave out an assignment, which started a soft grumbling by all students. The task was for us to write a five-hundred-word composition on what we were going to do in life after graduation. I was sort of displeased with the assignment and decided that I wasn't even going to try, then show up on Monday without my homework and see what would happen. Over that weekend, the thought of writing anything never even entered my mind, and when Monday came around, Mr. Frankel walked around the class to retrieve the compositions and didn't say a word to me about not having mine to hand over. The next day, I expected him to say something to me, but he didn't, and I then thought I was free and clear. That next Thursday, when the bell sounded to end the day, Mr. Frankel announced that he wanted to speak to me after class. Well, I had the feeling it was about not handing in my assignment and didn't know what to expect.

As the classroom emptied out, Mr. Frankel waited for everyone to leave, and at this point, I realized that I was the only one in the class who ignored his assignment. He asked me why I didn't write a composition, and I couldn't come up with a valid excuse and just shrugged my shoulders as if I could care less. Mr. Frankel then explained to me how important it was for me to start to realize what I was going to do in life after graduation. He was unaware of my situation at home and said that if I didn't know, he would choose for me! Mr. Frankel went on to say he enrolled me into a special after-school course at Central Commercial High School on Forty-Second Street in Manhattan. The course was called Traffic Management, and he had already spoken to the instructor and explained to me that if I missed any classes, he would be advised and I would not graduate. The classes were three days a week from 4:00 p.m. to 7:00 p.m. at night for which he then handed me a special free subway pass and said, "This will teach you to be something in life, and you'll never regret it." Mr. Frankel went as far as issuing me a special subway pass to be used for my trips to Manhattan, so I had no excuse for not to going.

That next Monday after school, I rode the subway to Manhattan and walked down Forty-Second Street and checked into the course along with about 150 other students from all over New York City.

We were divided into four groups, and my instructor was named Mr. Tyler who was an older teacher at Central Commercial High School and the key person in charge of the entire program. The sponsors of this program were the *New York Daily News* and *Traffic and Transportation Management* magazine, both based down the street from Central Commercial High School.

Mr. Tyler went on to explain what traffic management was, and it involved moving freight by truck, railroad, and airlines. He made his introduction very interesting and enlightened me that there was an industry that needed well-trained new workers, and college was not necessary. I was hooked and began to realize that I might have found my life's occupation, so I decided to never miss a class and pay close attention to Mr. Tyler and learn as much as I could. As the weeks came and went, certain students were dropping out, and I couldn't understand why, so I asked Mr. Tyler. He said it was expected and estimated that only about twenty-five of us students would finish the program and they would be smart enough to understand the true opportunity this was. I reported back to and thanked Mr. Frankel for doing what he did to make sure I became something and discovered a new beginning.

At the end of the course, the remaining twenty-four of us were helped to write a résumé, noting that we had just completed the Traffic Management program. Each student was asked to pick three companies from a list. It was explained to us that these companies were supporters of the program and needed workers who had some basic knowledge. From the list, I picked the New Jersey Zinc Company, US Freight Company, and Branch Motor Express and directed them to a certain person's attention as given to us by Mr. Tyler. We separately composed cover letters and attached them to our finished résumés and mailed them. Within four days, I received telegrams from each of the three companies I communicated with. The neighbors on the block thought someone had died in the family because of the Western Union deliveries. It was common in the early days of the Vietnam War to notify a family when their son, brother, or husband was killed, and they get notified by Western Union telegram. Each telegram I received revealed that they were interested in interviewing me for a position and to call the certain person noted.

My first interview was with US Freight located in downtown Manhattan on Houston Street, and I interviewed well and was offered a position in their piggyback section. I explained that I needed a few days to think it over since I already had an interview the next day with Branch Motor Express in Brooklyn. The second interview went even better than the first, and Branch Motor was a smaller growing company that was moving to Fifth Avenue in Manhattan within six months, and I decided that there was more learning to be had at Branch and accepted the offer. I started the Monday right after high school graduation and reported to work for the first time to a job that paid me to think and not for laboring.

By accepting the Branch Motor Express offer, I found myself very fortunate to have a job, since the Vietnam War held back young men in limbo. Corporations at that time were not hiring young men who had the military draft to look forward to. Many of my friends were told that they wouldn't be hired until they had completed their military obligation. So I thanked my lucky stars for having the opportunity for any company to even consider me for employment.

My first day at Branch, I reported to my department head, whose name was Hal Rexson, and sat with him at his desk where he began to describe what my duties were going to be. The office was situated in tight quarters, and the desks were equally close together. Hal laid out freight bills covering the top of his desk, and as we went through the billing structure of each freight bill, coffee break time came around with a wheeled cart that an outside vendor pushed about the office. We had our coffee and buttered roll and walked back to Hal's desk, placing the coffee cups on top of the freight bills. Just as Hal started to continue his overview, I reached over for a pen and knocked over both coffees all over the desktop, and Hal caught a wave in his lap, staining his suit pants. So here I was, within forty-five minutes of my first day at a real job and I gave my boss a coffee bath, wrecked the top of his desk, and attracted the attention of the whole department who were now all staring at me. I noticed Hal's facial expression wasn't a good one, and I felt like one big jerk when, at that point, someone in the department started to laugh, and it caused a reaction for all to join in on the laughter. When I looked back at Hal's face, I noticed he began laughing himself. Whenever the coffee cart came around for the next few weeks, everyone in the department would make sure to stand clear of me with a coffee cup in my hand.

About six months later, the company moved to Manhattan, making it a much easier commute for me by subway. The new offices were on Fifth Avenue and Sixteenth Street in a building that was quite elaborate for a trucking company while also creating many new positions to be filled. One of those new positions was a switchboard operator named Mary McLaughlin, who had a very upbeat personality and the looks that go with it. Mary and I were matched together by our coworkers, and we began dating on a now-and-then basis. She lived in the Bronx at 205th Street off the Concourse, which was the longest subway ride you could experience from the section of Brooklyn I lived in. I didn't and could not afford a car and had to rely on cabs and mass transit to get around. A few months later, Mary became a roommate with another beautiful coworker named Diana, and they set up an apartment on Ocean Parkway and Ditmas Avenue in Brooklyn, which was now only twenty minutes away from home. Mary and I began to see each other on a regular basis and were considered a couple. Chick did have a car, and we both would pick up Mary and Diana each morning for work, and he would drive us to downtown Brooklyn subway station to catch a train into Manhattan. This drive/subway method didn't really save any time, but if was a lot more fun than riding a subway all the way in to work each day.

In addition to working full time at Branch, I took a part-time job at Macy's in Herald Square, working in the Little Shop on the mezzanine level. This was a woman's department that sold mostly designer dresses, and one of my jobs was to remove the dresses that remained on racks after women tried them on. I had to announce on a small speaker system three times with a five-minute interval between announcements prior to walking down the aisle for garment pickups. This would allow women to finish their dressing so there would not be any embarrassing moments. For 98 percent of the women, it worked very well, but there were some who had no shame and completely ignored the announcements. Some of these customers left the curtains wide open or straight out asked me to help them zip up or down their dress, which I then had to explain was against Macy's rules. As a part-time employee of Macy's, it was mandatory to work on Thanksgiving Day in the famous parade.

My job at the 1965 Thanksgiving Day parade was as a line holder on a new balloon, Bullwinkle the Moose, who made its debut that year. It was explained to us line holders that Bullwinkle was the largest balloon ever displayed at the parade and we big guys had to "never let go of the lines no matter what." That Thanksgiving Day, the weather didn't help too much, because the winds were gusting at least forty miles per hour, and I had to report to upper Manhattan in the dark at 4:00 in the morning. When the parade finally started, the winds never diminished, and it was decided that the show would go on, and we began marching downtown. At about a mile down the parade route, a gust of wind came along and swept all the handlers holding the front of Bullwinkle, including me, about ten feet off the ground and hanging in the air. It felt as though we were going even higher, and when I looked down, it was at the point that if I let go, dropping from that height wouldn't be a good idea. Just as fast as the gust came, it diminished, and all frontline handlers dropped pretty quickly. The parade boss then rushed over and had extra reinforcement holders to double upon the lines, which worked, and we then proceeded to complete the route safely. I stayed at Macy's for another few weeks after that Thanksgiving of 1965, but it became a little too much for me to continue two jobs. Branch offered me the opportunity to stay an extra few hours a day and learn interstate commerce trucking rates on my time without any pay. This was what I was waiting for and couldn't let the opening pass me by, so I accepted the offer.

Hal Rexson took me aside and expressed how important it was to learn transportation rates if I wanted to make it in the freight transportation industry. Hal had the overcharge claims manager Bernie Tankensly, who was an older man, probably in his late fifties, with experience that was vast and covered decades of knowledge. I stayed after normal business hours for three days a week, and Bernie took the extra time and really explained to me the foundation needed to improve my career. Rating shipping charges was very technical, and the chance of errors was common. For the first time, I saw how third-party companies were auditing freight bills, and working on a contingency basis filing overcharge claims against the freight companies and receiving 50 percent of the mistakes found. It was a win-win situation for the company paying the freight charges, and the auditing companies were well compensated for their work. This experience opened my eyes to an entirely new presence in the industry I now chose for my career. Bernie turned out to be a close friend as the weeks and months passed, and he always took the extra step to clearly explain something that I didn't understand. We both spent many hours drinking beers after work at a local bar while I listened to Bernie tell me his stories of the trucking industry. Some of those stories still stand out in my memory while recalling them to help me make better business decisions during my career.

During this time, my staying to learn was interrupted by the New Year's Day transit strike of 1966, which lasted for twelve days and caused complete chaos. The strike effectively ended all service on the subway and buses in the city, affecting millions of commuters. The new mayor John Lindsay will always be remembered for having the union leader Michael Quill arrested and placed in jail for his leading the strike order, and only weeks later, Mike Quill passed away. As the true leader he was, Hal Rexson mapped out where everyone in his department lived and their proximity to the office. He created four car pools with himself as driver and the three other managers in the department as drivers. I was placed in Hal's car pool since he lived in the southern part of Queens, New York, not far from the Belt Parkway, and I would walk from home to a spot close to the Belt Parkway and meet him at 5:00 a.m. Hal then drove along his planned route, and we picked up three additional coworkers along the way. The route entailed going over the Verrazano Bridge to Staten Island then over the Bayonne Bridge and driving to Jersey City, New Jersey, where we would all pick up the Trans-Hudson tubes into Manhattan and walk the final blocks to the office. Each way would take about four to five hours. By the time I'd get home, it was time to go to bed and get up early the next morning and start it all over again. We all couldn't wait for the strike to come to an end, and when it did, it was a joyful moment.

In September 1966, Chick married his childhood sweetheart Veronica "Ronnie" Petrone, who lived a few blocks away on West Seventh Street. While Chick and Ronnie were dating, there were many times when he would have Frank and me walk him to Ronnie's house, and the two of us would turn around and head back to West Tenth Street. Sometimes on the way home, we could scrounge enough between us to stop at L&B Spumoni Gardens for a spumoni or Italian ice. This routine became common place, especially during pleasant whether when Frank and I didn't have anything better to do. Chick and Ronnie made the picture-perfect couple while Ronnie's family was the complete opposite of Chick's. It seemed that there was always a party going on and nothing but good family fun between all. Ronnie's dad died when she was young, and her mother, Carrie, with the help of her sister Annie and brother-in-law Jimmie had to work and raise three daughters without a father. Any outsider would have never guessed what Ronnie's family situation was just by observing her sisters, aunts, uncles, and cousins every day. A perfect family description would be close-knit since they all lived so nearby and continued to always stay together as a unit even when relocating came into play. Most of Ronnie's family picked up and moved to Staten Island, which was the new frontier of New York City when the Verrazano Bridge was opened. Vast amounts of untouched woodlands in only New York City standards were available, and entire new communities were built for all those Brooklynites wanting to plant new roots.

A few days a week, especially on Friday nights, some of the Branch workers would meet at a local bar named Thirteen East, which was located at Thirteenth East Sixteenth Street. The bar was owned by the International Machinist Union with their headquarters just around the corner. The bar was a hangout for the union hierarchy, and when I look back now, we were hardly ever charged for food and drink. The way it worked was that Eddie, the bartender, would take out the cost for the first round of drink and leave the change on the bar. Management was fully aware of this and always gave the OK nod to Eddie. Food was arranged and brought out from the kitchen on a buffet basis, and you could eat all you wanted without any cost. Even the jukebox didn't require any money to play music. I felt that the place was a front for the union, and they needed an appearance as a real establishment. The union types that hung out looked like Mafia characters of the 1950s and certainly gave the impression that there was something else going on.

Ronnie & Chick

The head union guy was called Sal, and he once offered me a job to work for a large car rental company at $500 a week. At that time, I was only making seventy dollars a week, so I was very interested in making more and asked what the job entailed. Sal took me in the corner of the bar with an individual I assume was his bodyguard friend and described in a low tone of voice that I would reposition cars for the rental company between Idlewild (JFK Airport) and LaGuardia Airport, and every once in a while, a package would be placed in the trunk of the car and that I should never ask any questions, just drive. Suddenly I realized that I was placing myself into a corner by asking that question. My thinking jumped ahead, and all I could see was the corrupt outcome of an old gangster movie playing. I expressed my thanks to Sal for thinking of me, but his bodyguard gave me a dirty look. I quickly explained that I would rather stay where I was and learn an honest occupation. His eyebrows at that point raised, signaling he didn't understand my reasoning, so I had to gently walk it back to all the time and effort I placed into learning what I had. Sal stood about six feet four inches tall, and he placed his arm over my shoulder and said if I changed my mind, the job would always be available if I wanted it. With those words, I felt relieved, because the last thing I wanted to do was to have him take it the wrong way since I knew people like him and his bodyguard friend didn't take rejection well. Sal had no idea what I was making in salary, and I never mentioned it, and if he did know, my rejection would have not been taken so well.

My girlfriend, Mary, was an excellent singer, and she loved to perform in front of an audience, and Thirteen East gladly gave her that opportunity. On Friday nights, only a piano entertainer played special requests, allowing her to sing her heart away, requesting one Irish song after another. While she sang, she'd walk around the bar and sing to the patrons and occasionally sit on their laps by invitation. I made it clear that she was asking for trouble and it wasn't a good idea to do what she was doing, especially with people like this. Mary would pay no attention to me and continued her singing routine whether I liked it or not. One Friday night, another coworker named Terri Kandybowicz just so happened to stop by Thirteen East to meet with all of us and have a drink. Mary was running late, and Terri sat next to me, and we started a conversation about this being her first time at Thirteen East. She explained that she recently received a Dear John letter from her boyfriend, Mike, who was serving in the army during the Vietnam War. Terri's boyfriend wouldn't allow her to go out while he was away, and this was her first time out since the letter. I explained to Terri that just a few days before, I had joined the navy and was scheduled to leave for submarine training sometime in January 1967. We both then continued to talk about the Vietnam War and the draft and the effects it all had on everyone's life.

At that juncture, I explained that someone I knew recently was killed in Vietnam, named Mark Sivatta, a marine corps PFC. It was reported in the *New York Daily News* on June 18, 1966, that he triggered a land mine, and both his legs were blown off and he survived four more days before dying. Mark was a rough and tough guy who had no fear. He was a member in a boxing club in the neighborhood. One day after dinner in the summer of 1962, Chick and I were sitting in the kitchen when Mark barged in, demanding that I go and box in his boxing gym. He wouldn't take no for an answer. The expression on his face was sincere, and I couldn't figure out why he chose me, so I asked him, and he said to me someone named Tony in my ninth-grade class suggested it to him. I knew whom he was referring to, and I wasn't pleased. Subsequently, I talked my way out by saying that I would give Tony my answer, which Mark accepted. As it all turned out, after school, I waited for Tony to come out, and when he did, I started to let him know what happened as my anger took over. I started to beat him with a rolled-up newspaper. Tony didn't put up much of a fight that day, and he clearly understood when it was over that Mark Sivatta should never again barge into my house.

December 7, 1966, the twenty-fifth anniversary of Pearl Harbor, I joined the US Navy after ample advice from another former high school teacher named Mr. Bloom, whom we students called Chief Bloom. Ever since I was a kid, I was infatuated by submarines. Chief Bloom was a former WWII veteran and submariner. With Chief Bloom's blessing, I joined a special program that would give me the opportunity of fulfilling a childhood dream and be a part of the US Navy Submarine Service.

I was about to be drafted into the army, so I figured if I was going to serve my country, I would serve on my terms. The draft was being pushed hard, and many of my friends had various types of deferments such as going to college, being married, or expecting a baby. There were one hundred of us volunteering that night, and everyone had their parents and family present for the swearing-in ceremony except me. In the audience, there were a handful of navy veterans who actually served at Pearl Harbor during the attack, and they gave us recruits a brief overview of the events that followed. Some of the stories that were told to the group gave me chills and made me one very proud American that night, making it a day that will always live in my memory. Two days later, I received a letter from my draft board, and I felt the lower left-hand corner of the envelope, which turned out to be only one subway token instead of two. All

New York City residents received subway passage by token to get to and from their draft boards. My first letter from the draft board for my health physical included two subway tokens taped in the inside left-hand corner of the envelope. Without even opening the envelope, the single token meant that it was a final notice, and it would get me to the draft board, and I didn't need a return token because I wouldn't be coming home for a while. I handed the letter over to the navy, and they explained that under my contract, I was all theirs and the notice would be cancelled.

The conversation with Terri lasted a while, and Mary finally showed up and noticed our sitting together, but instead of saying hello, she walked right past me and went directly to the piano player and started to perform her routine again just like nothing ever happened. Mary never once looked my way, and I tried to get her attention with no luck. I then told Terri that I was leaving and motioned to Mary who again paid no attention to me leaving the bar. The next day, Mary's roommate Dianna called me and invited me down to a different restaurant around the corner, and unknown to me, she had Mary with her. The discussion was all about what happened the night before and how Mary felt betrayed by me when she noticed me sitting with Terri. I explained that I was just waiting for her to arrive and Terri and I were just having a simple conversation about the Vietnam War and being drafted. It then came to me that here I was, explaining myself for no reason, and she could sing and sit on laps all night while I had to watch. I made up my mind quickly that I no longer wanted any part her and the relationship. I stood up and said to Mary "Have a good life" and walked out of the restaurant and never looked back.

Another coworker invited all of us in the traffic department to a Christmas party at his home, which included Mary and Terri as guests. It felt a little awkward being at a party and neither Mary nor I speaking to each other. I walked over to Terri and drummed up a conversation, and when a song we both liked began playing, I asked her to slow-dance. About an hour into the party, the record player began slipping, and the results were not sounding too good. Our friend Dave, our host, didn't have another record player, so I said I did and that I lived only twenty minutes away by car. The only person who came by car was Terri, so it worked out great for both of us, and we left the party and headed to my grandma's to pick up the record player. As Terri was driving and we were crossing over Ocean Parkway, I told her to make a left turn, and she did but made it too soon, and we ended up on the horse path that ran parallel to the service road before the turn. Back then, riders on horseback were allowed to ride along Ocean Parkway almost from one end to the other. The horse path was a narrow, bumpy dirt road, and Terri couldn't turn around, so we had to drive for another block before we could exit the path. I started to laugh hard, and Terri was a little embarrassed at first, but once she gave it some thought, she also had a good laugh too. We both continued to Grandma's house.

When we arrived, as we both walked in, I noticed my father with Pat on one of his infrequent visits, sitting at the kitchen table with Grandma Rose and my uncle Curly. Since it was only my second time meeting Pat, I also felt uncomfortable, but I introduced Terri to the group. I explained that we couldn't stay and that we only came for a record player, but the conversation kept going, and this time Pat had much more to say and really opened up the conversation. They all thought that Terri was my girlfriend and continued to ask how we met and that we made a great-looking couple. I think that Terri was embarrassed again and didn't know how to answer some of their questions, so I had to jump in a few times to clear the air. Terri and I finally left and went back to the party while everyone was wondering what took us so long, and the group hinted that we must have stopped for some lovemaking along the way. We both looked at each other and gave a smirk and giggled as though it was our very own secret.

Terri and I began dating on a regular basis, and oftentimes the traveling by subway from Greenpoint to Gravesend was not a joyride, to say the least, especially late at night. During that winter, most trains didn't have heat, and the Smith and Ninth street station had an outdoor elevated platform. The station stood about two hundred feet above the Gowanus Canal, and the winds ripped through your bones just standing there.

JOE ROSATO

On a cool April Friday night in 1967, after drinking and eating at Thirteen East with Terri and returning her home to Greenpoint, I walked the five long blocks to the *G* train subway station entrance on India Street. The much closer entrance on Franklin Street closes at 11:00 p.m., and it was now 2:00 a.m. in the morning and I was on my way home to Gravesend. I boarded the *G* train, and I noticed that I was the only passenger on the train, so I took a seat and leaned against the window as I had done many times before. On the second stop, which was Lorimer Street, the doors opened, and I heard loud talking noise. Looking up, I saw about ten black males, and they all started to sit around the same area I was sitting even though the train was empty. The *G* train travels through some real tough neighborhoods in Brooklyn, and I hadn't experienced any conditions like this before. It only took a minute, and they started to talk in third person about me, saying, "What's this white boy doing in our seat?" and "Does his mama know where he is?" Fear started to enter my mind, and I was looking for a way to resolve or neutralize the situation. Suddenly I heard a familiar deep, strong voice say, "Leave him alone, he's a friend." I looked over to see where that deep voice was coming from, and I noticed someone standing off to the side who appeared to be the leader, standing about six feet four inches and weighing at least 350 pounds. He spoke directly to me and said, "How are you doing Joe?" I looked up, and then it struck me that it was Howie Springer from the eighth grade. The group paid close attention to what Howie said, and their attitudes completely changed. Howie told them what I had done in a fight and how I had helped him when I didn't have to. I then stood up, and Howie motioned me to sit next to him, away from his friends, and then explained that he had to quit school and work because his mother needed support. His family moved away and relocated to the Bedford-Stuyvesant section of Brooklyn where jobs were more available for a black guy. I reminisced about his wearing a suit to school every day, and he said it was his mother's rule to look his best at all times. We also talked about his athletic abilities and our playing volleyball in gym where our class always won because of the slamming spikes our opponents couldn't return.

The *G* train arrived at the Smith and Ninth Street station, which was the last stop, and I had to change for the *F* train for the final ride home. Howie and his buddies all gathered round and insisted they stay with me until the *F* train arrived. We then said our final good-byes, and they all walked down the subway platform toward the street level. It all ended with a lot of admiration for each other and the fact that we would probably never see each other again. All this gave me a strange feeling that Howie was in a certain place in his life that he couldn't get out of. As they walked out of view, I knew that the situation would have been like a bad dream if Howie weren't there, probably resulting in me being robbed, beaten, or both.

At this point, I began to look at Terri very differently, and she seemed to feel the same way about me. My uncle Curly would constantly ask me about Terri whenever he had the chance even though he had only met her for a short time. He was the first to tell me that Terri was the one for me. He was 100 percent right as it turned out Terri and I started dating steady and both fell in love pretty quickly thereafter. Grandma Rose also got along very well with Terri and, in her own funny way, would always compare her to Mary, and she would say, "You are now lucky to have her," which made me feel as though I was in a special place.

Only a few weeks later, I said my good-byes to Terri and the family, and I left on February 5, 1967, for my submarine training in New London, Connecticut. I gathered at Grand Central Station with about forty other recruits, and we boarded a train for New London, taking about three hours to reach our destination. It was an extremely cold day waiting for the navy shuttle to pick us up at the train station, and when it did arrive, I remember there not being any heat in the bus. When we got to the base, there were all kinds of security checks since New London was the headquarters for building and operating our nation's nuclear submarine fleet around the world. Most of the training involved classroom sessions about electricity and how submarines run under operations. Physical requirements came into the picture along the way, which included a fifty-foot-deep dive tank that we had to transcend from the bottom, wearing a mask that only had one breath of air. Each recruit entered a chamber that was flooded and had to make his way out and up to the surface. Along the side of the tank, there were divers available if needed for air or any other type of assistance.

The training period was three months long, and upon completion, I was given preliminary orders to serve on the USS *Nautilus* (SSN-571), which was my childhood dream since the movie *20,000 Leagues under the Sea* was released in 1954 by Walt Disney. All I had remaining was to pass one last physical and then receive my final orders to serve for two years' active duty. The USS *Nautilus* was planned and personally supervised by Admiral Hyman G. Rickover, being built in nearby Groton, Connecticut. It was commissioned on September 30, 1954, making it the world's first nuclear-powered submarine. On August 3, 1958, the *Nautilus* became the first submarine to complete a submerged transit under the North Pole. By 1967, there were many more modern and larger submarines in our nation's fleet, but none as historical as the *Nautilus*.

My last physical didn't go too well, and it was detected that my blood pressure escalated far beyond the standards while under compression. I was immediately transferred to St. Albans Naval Hospital in Queens, New York, for testing and observation by placing me in a general heart ward. During my stay, Terri visited me whenever she had the chance, and it looked like the navy was going to discharge me, and once again I would be subject to the draft. During a discharge interview with the medical director of St. Albans, I was given the option of being transferred to the regular navy, which gave me the opportunity to serve on any other type of navy ship except a submarine. I took the offer and reported to my navy reserve center where I had to be retrained, which would take a few more months to accomplish.

Because of my now long-delayed active duty, Terri and I decided to be married before my two years began. We set the date of January 13, 1968, and started to plan our lives accordingly for the future. The first thing that had to be dealt with was whether my parents would play some sort of a role in our married lives, and I had to make the first steps for forgiveness. Terri insisted that we both make amends and visit my dad and Pat initially in their Manhattan apartment and forgive him for past events and invite them both to our wedding. My mother had just recently married herself for the third time to Al St. Cyr and was living in North Bergen, New Jersey, and we decided to meet them in the Bus Stop Restaurant, also in Manhattan. Al asked me who the best man was, and I informed him it would probably be Chick, and that's when my mother once again made the comment, "Just like the soup." I then couldn't help but ask again what she meant by that. Mom gave the same answer I heard many times before: silence.

Both my parents really didn't understand what Terri and I were trying to accomplish during our visits, and neither one of them opened up and asked for any forgiveness. This was in complete dissimilarity from Terri's family when they received the news of our getting married. But I have to say, both my parents were equally happy that we made the effort to include them in our wedding activities.

We decided to rent an apartment on Avenue T in my old neighborhood of Gravesend and decorated it even knowing that it would be a short-term stay for me since I had to leave for military duty. Once I had to leave, Terri would stay and continue working at a New York City law firm as a legal secretary. My in-laws, John and Virginia, were happy to pay for our wedding reception, which was held at the Polonaise Terrace in Greenpoint, Brooklyn. We had 250 guests, and the celebration went on till the wee hours of that night on January 13, 1968. We became husband

Our Wedding

and wife, and I found at that moment the love of my life. Chick was of course my best man, and Ronnie accepted to be Terri's maid of honor after Terri's best friend, Loraine, backed out at the last minute. Terri never forgot what Ronnie did for us by stepping in as maid of honor, and she became a very close family member after that. The reception was so well accepted by both relatives and friends that we constantly were given rave reviews for many years to come.

But there were also some glitches that temporarily stole the moment, and among them was that the photographer didn't realize there was no film in his camera while taking photos at Terri's home with her parents and siblings. The second problem was the wedding favors spelled Terri's name as Theresa and not the correct spelling of Teresa. The biggest glitch happened toward the end of the reception when Terri and I were leaving to spend that night at the International Hotel at JFK Airport, since we had a very early flight leaving in the morning for our honeymoon in San Juan, Puerto Rico. I prearranged to have Chick and Ronnie drive us to JFK, but since Chick owned a VW beetle, four people and luggage wouldn't make it. Frank was also in the wedding party as an usher and volunteered to follow us in his VW beetle and carry the overflow luggage that couldn't fit in Chick's car. Both VWs left, and we entered the Brooklyn–Queens Expressway I-278, which was under major construction, and Frank could not keep up, and we became separated. Chick slowed down, trying to have Frank catch up, but he was nowhere in sight. Frank had Terri's luggage in his car, and he had absolutely no idea where we were staying that night at JFK. When we arrived at the hotel, we were hoping that Frank might already be there, with no such luck. Once checked in, I started to call anyone connected to Frank, trying to get a message to him, and it took hours, but it didn't work. Terri and I still hadn't slept a wink, wondering about her luggage, and at about 3:00 in the morning, the room phone rang. It was Frank calling from home, asking me how I was going to get the luggage he had. He also described his driving around for hours and stopping at numerous hotels within the JFK Airport complex, checking to see if we were registered as quests. Frank obviously missed the first biggest hotel you see when entering the airport. I clearly explained that he had to, without any hesitation, deliver all the luggage to the front-desk clerk at the International Hotel ASAP since we were leaving in only two and a half hours. We then tried to get some sleep at least for a couple of hours and prayed that the luggage would be at the front desk in the morning. As it turned out, when we awoke at 5:00 a.m., I quickly called the front desk and asked if the luggage arrived, and the clerk replied not to his knowledge, but I noticed that it was a different person from 3:00 a.m. whom I spoke to. We then walked out to the front desk and searched for ourselves. In the meantime, the person who was on duty at 3:00 a.m. called in to advise that he forgot to mention, to our relief, that the luggage was stored in a certain holding room. It was music to our ears, and I think I could have jumped over the front desk and kissed the clerk thank-you.

Our honeymoon was the first time for both of us flying, and our flight left right on time via Pan Am Airways nonstop to San Juan. We chose the Conch Hotel, which was a beautiful place situated on the beach in the then newer section of San Juan. The hotel had a major theater, and we saw on separate nights Bobby Darin in his closing performance and Connie Francis in her opening-night performance. Our central location made it easy to walk to most of the finest restaurants and casinos San Juan had to offer. Terri and I had a most outstanding honeymoon and gathered countless memories that we continually recollected for years to come.

After a week of honeymooning in San Juan, it was our plan to spend another week at a ski lodge in New Hampshire, but while in Puerto Rico, a message was relayed to me from my navy reserve center in Brooklyn to call immediately. I knew it wouldn't be any good news, so I called and spoke to the person that left the message. A few seconds later, I was informed that the following week, I was to report to the USS *Bristol* (DD-857) stationed at the Brooklyn Navy Yard for a two-week training in the Atlantic Ocean. The *Bristol* was a WWII navy destroyer that was being used for training missions, and it was just coming off a major renovation project. I knew that this interruption in my life was the way it was going to be as long as I had that two-year active duty hanging over my head.

I reported for duty and was given the joyous job of mess cooking, which was just another name for dish and pot washer. Ship and crew departed the Brooklyn Navy Yard exactly on time and cruised to Hamilton, Bermuda. It was my first venture on a ship in the open seas of the Atlantic Ocean, and I quickly found out that old navy destroyers don't ride the waves too well. The seas were so rough that except for the brief time spent in the town of Hamilton, I was seasick around the clock and still had to perform the job of mess cooking. One morning on the third day, I reported to sick bay for medical attention, thinking that there might be something available to help the wicked symptoms of seasickness. A navy corpsman described that there were two items he could give me to help: one was a pack of saltine crackers and the other was a bucket for vomiting. I took the two items he handed me and walked back to the galley in total frustration. It then passed through my mind, "What if I was permanently stationed on a destroyer for my two years' active duty?" Over the next few months that followed, I kept my fingers firmly crossed and hoped that somehow it wouldn't happen to me.

The two-week *Bristol* ordeal finally finished, but I couldn't leave the ship until a final inspection was made of the galley, which took a few extra hours. When I finally arrived a few hours late at our apartment, I found that Terri had cooked our first meal as a married couple, but the delay caused the pork chops to be reheated many times, causing them to be overcooked and tasting like shoe leather. But knowing that she really tried hard to make it a special first dinner and that we were now living in our very own new apartment made the well-done pork chops easy to swallow. We both commuted each workday together into Manhattan. I would get out of work earlier than her and walk uptown so we could meet and ride home together.

Shortly after we were married and living in our apartment, we invited my in-laws over for Sunday dinner, and Terri made homemade meat lasagna, which she prepared the day before and refrigerated uncooked. Her mother and father loved Italian cooking, and it was meant to be a real special meal. The lasagna was baked in the oven and was served with antipasto salad and meatballs. Everything was ready, and after a few drinks, we sat down in our little kitchen, and Terri served the lasagna. As soon as I tasted the lasagna, I noticed a funny taste in my mouth and looked at Terri for direction, and she bit into it and also made a weird face. It was then discovered that the lasagna went sour overnight in the refrigerator, and it was not edible. Terri called my grandma Rose and found out that you never prepare lasagna and refrigerate it uncooked because the egg used inside turns bad. She should have fully cooked the lasagna the day before and reheated it the next day. Terri learned from experience many things about cooking after we were married and became an accomplished cook whom family and friends would always consult for directions.

We decided that a newer car in our married lives would be a blessing instead of taking subways and relying on an old beat-up 1962 Chrysler 300 my father-in-law gave Terri, which always had a recurring front-end problem that could never be fixed correctly. Part of our wedding proceeds was used to purchase a new red 1968 VW Karmann Ghia, which was a sporty two-door version that barely had a backseat that folded down for storage. The Ghia looked like a million bucks with the color red that gave it an Italian sports car appearance. Since Chick, Frank, and a few other friends already owned VW vehicles that they called reliable and economical, it made the brand what we were looking for. The 1968 Ghia had the first automatic stick shift, which allowed the driver to shift gears manually or automatically. It also was the first model to offer an FM radio, which really changed music listing habits for a long time to come.

The Karmann Ghia was my second love, and being the first car I ever owned made it my prized posession. Driving and handling that car gave me a true feeling of a European sports car with each drive I took while also reproducing a zesty driving sensation. My favorite photo is Terri dressed in a light-gray chemise dress, black high-heel shoes, sporting her first short haircut with her blonde hair shining in the sunlight. All these Karmann Ghia memories would somehow be fated.

"Patience is not simply the ability to
wait-it's how we behave while we're waiting."

—Joyce Meyer

CHAPTER 9

—And pain is all around.

The next few months went by quickly, and before I knew it, I received my orders for active duty, and we both felt relieved and sad at the same time. My navy orders were to report to pier 12 in Naval Operating Base (NOB) Norfolk, Virginia, being assigned to the navy's newest aircraft carrier, the USS *America* (CVA-66). The orders didn't state any other information, but I knew enough to realize that when aircraft carriers leave their home port, they don't return for quite a while. The good side told us that the sooner I served, the sooner it would be all over, and our lives would be able to live out their destiny without any further disruptions. Advising my employer AR Traffic Consultants that I was finally being activated was met with no surprise, and I was promised my position back when I returned. The company gave me a going-away luncheon party, and I said my good-byes to everyone. I had to leave Terri on March 4, 1968, and we both decided to say our good-byes at our apartment instead of at the airport, and taking a taxi was more tolerable than her driving me. The night before I left, I couldn't sleep at all, and neither could Terri. We both tossed and turned, and I could hear her so slightly weeping during that night.

On the very early morning of March 4, I called a local taxi company and informed them my flight left at 8:00 a.m. and they would need to pick me up at 6:00 a.m. At that time of the morning from Gravesend, it would only take about forty-five minutes to arrive at JFK, giving me plenty of time to check in. Terri was trembling at this point, and all we could do was hug each other very tight while kissing and hoping for the best. A car's headlight appeared outside our ground-floor apartment, and I looked out the window and saw that the taxi had arrived. I never will forget that last kiss, and it seemed to give me a special boost of spirit, knowing that I had something so very special to come home to when it was all over. I grabbed my fully packed sea bag and tossed it over my shoulder, walked to the door, and turned while taking in one last look at Terri. She was still wearing her pink polka-dot pajamas with a tissue in hand, sniffling and tears running down her cheeks. I said, "I love you, and I will always love you," and I opened the door and walked outside over to the waiting taxi at the curb, and we then pulled away. I told the driver to make a right turn on West Tenth Street so we could pass Grandma Rose's house one last time before leaving, and while moving down the block, I recalled all the fond memories of living there. My imagination ran away, recalling those stickball and hit-the-container games I played with Chick, Frank, and the guys on the block, and it brought a smile to my face. The driver then asked me what airline, and I told him

USS America

National Airlines, and we snaked through the neighborhood on to the Belt Parkway toward JFK Airport.

The driver noticed I was dressed in uniform and asked me where I was headed for. I explained that I was flying to Norfolk to meet a ship and didn't know where I would finally end up. The driver then looked up into the rearview mirror and said to me, "That's a bummer, sailor." It was the very first time I heard myself being addressed as a sailor and began wondering how many more times I would hear the phrase over the next two years.

During the short flight, I couldn't stop thinking of Terri and hoped that she would be able to cope with the loneliness and have her family to morally support her. I took a good look around the plane and noticed many other sailors also dressed in uniform and wondered how each of their lives was being interrupted for military service. When the plane landed, an announcement was made that the Navy had shuttle buses outside the terminal for those who were going to NOB. When I located my sea bag at the luggage carousel, I was instructed to take it outside to a truck parked next to bus number 1 for NOB. The ride on an old-type school bus painted battleship gray was about thirty minutes, and when the bus turned toward pier 12, I took in a real good look and felt the massive size of the *America* moored to that pier. Her size alone was mind-boggling, measuring 1,200 feet in length with a 4½ square football field area for a flight deck and a conning tower stretching into the sky at over 225 feet high from ground level. A weird emotion came over me at that instant when I realized that this colossal ship was now my home and I would be sharing it with 5,200 other navy personnel. I also knew that other ships were named after cities, states, senators, our founding fathers, and presidents. But only the *America* was named after this great country she served.

It turned out that the entire busload of sailors were for the *America*, and we all assembled in the hangar bay for special instructions. The hangar bay is another immense area inside the ship, which stores all the aircraft for the flight squadrons. There were about eighty-five fixed-wing aircraft with a few helicopters aboard the *America*, and you can only imagine the size of the area needed to logistically move that amount of aircraft around. The ship was also equipped with three extremely large elevators that were capable of lifting at least two planes each at the same time to and from the flight deck within only a few seconds. I observed a lot of hustle and bustle going on among the crew, who were loading hundreds of shrink wrapped pallets, and I sensed that something big was about to happen.

Each of us was then given our duty divisions to report to, and mine being First Division as a boatswain's mate. The job of being a boatswain's mate was a totally new experience for me since the job entailed working with deck equipment, boat seamanship and rigging. This all gave me something more to wonder about. Just when my wondering took hold, the announcement "Attention on deck" was made, and the executive officer of the ship was introduced as Commander Chew, who went into a clear and precise description of what was about to happen. He stated that the next morning the *America* was bound for her first tour in the Vietnam War. The voyage to Vietnam and back involved circling the world at the same time since our massive size wouldn't allow her to fit through the Panama Canal. We would sail south, crossing the equator with a brief stop in Rio de Janeiro, Brazil, and then continue east across the South Atlantic Ocean to Cape Town, South Africa, for another brief stop, and before cruising across the Indian Ocean, into the South China Sea with a stop at Subic Bay, Republic of the Philippines. Once at Subic Bay, the *America* would pick up the last of what was needed and finally arrive at Yankee Station as flagship of the US Seventh Fleet in the Gulf of Tonkin off the coast of North Vietnam. Yankee Station was the official name given by the navy for a staging place in the air war, and it included at least five aircraft carriers and their support ships.

The two major bases used by US forces during the Vietnam War were Clark Air Force Base and Subic Bay Naval Base situated next to each other in the Philippines. From Yankee Station, the US Navy delivered 60 percent of all the bombs dropped in the war and organized it from numerous aircraft carriers and one battleship, the USS *New Jersey*. Our military allies in the region, namely, the Philippines and Japan, wouldn't allow any US war planes to take off or land if they were bombing Vietnam. So the navy, having its own floating air fields on water called aircraft carriers, answered the call. In the Gulf of Tonkin, unlike previous wars fought, the US Navy controlled the air and sea space, so aircraft carriers and battleships had no menace to fear.

Commander Chew closed out his speech, welcoming us. We were taken to each of our duty divisions by escorts since the knowledge and layout of this massive ship were very compelling. We walked forward in the hangar bay toward the bow of the ship and climbed a few staircases zigging and zagging to higher levels. We reached First Division's sleeping compartment, and I was handed over to a third-class petty officer (PO) and told to stand there and wait for the leading first-class petty officer (PO). While I was waiting there, the sleeping compartment cleaning person with mop and bucket in hand was trying to do his job and was being heckled by other shipmates making fun of his Puerto Rican accent. There were four other shipmates calling out "Archie Garcia, you're a Spic" and laughing their heads off. This went on for a few minutes when suddenly Archie came straight at me and threw a punch toward my face, but I bobbed and the punch missed. I then grabbed his small-framed body and placed him in a bear-hug hold while the other shipmates began to yell out "Fight! Fight!" Quickly the sleeping compartment door opened, and the leading PO rushed in and witnessed me, the new guy, holding his compartment cleaner in a dominant wrestling hold. The other four shipmates rushed to break it up as if they were just innocent bystanders. The four shipmates took me to the leading PO's office located on the forecastle section and introduced me to L. James, BM1 (boatswain's mate first class), an African American who was a lifer in the navy with over twenty years of service.

On the way to the office, I started thinking that I was going to get blamed for something I didn't do, and it looked like my first impression wasn't a good one. James was now sitting at his desk and had my orders and file in front of him and looked up and said, "I noticed you're from Brooklyn. We have rules here that you are not aware of, and if you have a chip on your shoulder about Puerto Ricans, you must have the same opinion of other racial minorities."

I then explained that when I entered the sleeping compartment, there were others calling out racial comments and Archie lunged at me for no reason whatsoever. James took a long, hard look at me and said, "I will get to know you real well in the coming months, and I'll keep my eye on you, sailor," and he then introduced me to his right-hand man, T. Moody, BM2 (boatswain's mate second class), also an African American navy lifer with twenty years of service who would be my work detail leader for the future. Moody gave me an awkward look and told me to follow him into the forecastle, where he handed me a bucket, sponge, and cleanser and told me to start washing down the white bulkheads. I, at that time, felt that my next two years were going to be hell, and the people in charge of me thought I was a racist. This really upset me.

My first day on the *America* came to an end in a way I never expected in any stretch of my imagination, so I decided to make the best of things and somehow change the first impressions that were forced upon my arrival. The next morning, reveille was sounded, and while walking to the galley through the hangar bay, I heard band music coming from pier 12. I stopped and looked out, and there were a couple of thousand family dependents standing in the cold, waving and singing "God Bless America." It gave me goose bumps, hearing that song for the first time sung to a ship named after the country it served. The lyrics of "God Bless America" contributed a new meaning of a great song as well as sanctifying our mission. The USS *America* was now officially on its way to be a part of the Vietnam War.

The only communication with home from here on out was writing and receiving letters, which took about two weeks to deliver home and two weeks for the reply to arrive. Since we were in a war zone, all letters mailed back home were marked in the upper right-hand corner as "Free," no postage needed. This made any questions concerning family activities very difficult to grasp since it took at least a month to fully receive an answer. Finding time to write was a problem because assigned duties and watches always got in the way. The formal workday started at 7:00 a.m. and went until 4:00 p.m., and in addition, a four-hour duty watch after working hours was mandatory. To help complicate matters, a sea detail each day of taking on fuel, food, or supplies would be arranged by meeting a supply/tanker ship at sea and transferring hoses and lines to exchange cargo/fuel. At times, these sea details went on for many hours, and the supply ship would have to travel alongside the *America* while both ships were moving in the same direction, leaving only a short (dangerous) distance between them.

My assigned duty watch station was the bridge, and I began training for the helmsman and lee helmsman positions. The bridge is the control center where all communications, navigation, and flight commands are made. It's also the location where the captain controls and commands the ship along with, in our case, being a flagship, the admiral, who commands the fleet. These positions of helmsman and lee helmsman involved controlling the speed and steering the ship, and both were on-the-job training positions. Once qualified, you had to carefully listen and repeat out loud any command actions by the officer of the deck. Keeping the *America* on a steady speed and course was of the utmost importance since the slightest deviation created a hazard for aircraft takeoffs and landings. Each aircraft needed as much lift as possible, and the ship would always head directly into the wind while the catapults within a short distance propelled the aircraft at two hundred miles per hour before departing the flight deck.

Standing watches on the bridge were educational and enjoyable while controlling the speed and driving the biggest man-made mechanism in the world presented me with an existence of honor. I became very good at what I did on the bridge and began to be requested at the helm during sea replenishment details, which were at times some nail-biting experiences. It was clearly explained to me that just a few months earlier, there was an accident involving another aircraft carrier's elevators ripping open the side of a supply ship. The accident occurred because the two ships were allowed to get too close to each other during windy conditions. Keeping two large ships within just a few feet of each other steadily while traveling parallel at sea with changing current and wind conditions wasn't an easy job to do, but I constantly considered it a challenge and completed all assignments without any incidents.

The ship's preparation for crossing the equator began to take hold following the longstanding naval traditions. It was customary that all pollywogs (those who never crossed) be initiated by shellbacks (those who have crossed) over at least an eight-hour period, which included some nasty things. It all started by crawling through decomposed food garbage shoots while walking on all fours as a dog on a leash, kissing and pressing your face into the greased belly of the fattest man on board, plus constantly being whipped in the ass with torn fire hoses. There was also banging metal buckets placed over your head and being dunked over the side of the ship for a final wash-down and bath. I might add that during the dunking event, marines were carefully placed, armed with M-16 rifles to shoot at any sharks that approached the submerged cargo nets. Somehow, that day about 1,800 pollywog enlisted men and officers passed the naval tradition and became shellbacks under the order of Neptunus Rex, who is the mythical leader of the raging sea.

We arrived at Rio de Janeiro, and the first thing I did after stepping ashore was run and find somewhere to call Terri at home. After asking around, I was directed to a communication center, where for twenty dollars per five minutes—cash up front—I was able to place a call back home using a headset radio. I calculated the timing so Terri would be home to pick up the call. The call was placed, and I overheard the ring and prayed to myself she would be there. On the second or third ring, Terri picked up, and hearing her voice sounded like music to my ears. She was surprised by the call, and I explained that we only had five minutes to speak, so we tried to keep it quick and cover the really important things. We must have told each other how much we loved each other a dozen times before hearing an operator telling us that the five minutes were over. That call alone made me feel so satisfied it gave me the energy to continue on the long road ahead without worrying about home.

During the visit to Rio, I just so happened to run into Moody and James in a bar and walked up to them, buying them a round of drinks. While sipping on our drinks, I thought it was a good time to bring up what happened with Archie and me being accused of calling him a Spic. James jumped in and described Archie as a person who was constantly being made fun of by all and he was very frustrated about it. I learned through James that Archie late that day went to him and explained what really happened in the sleeping compartment. Moody and James at this time both were completely at ease with me and explained that I was a good addition to First Division, which made me very pleased and relaxed.

Cruising from Rio to Cape Town, South Africa, entailed a journey through the southern part of the Atlantic Ocean, which is a vast wilderness of sea water covering thousands of nautical miles. The only sign of life I saw was an occasional whale in the distance and seagulls whenever the fantail was opened. Opening the fantail was an announcement of the ability of certain assigned personnel to throw trash and garbage over the rear of the ship. It was an amazing sight to see when one minute there was not a glimpse of any land or gulls and the next moment, when garbage hit the water, hundreds of gulls were coming from nowhere and making their descent to attack the trash. This was also a time when some of the marines on board ship would hold target practice shooting at the floating trash bags and cause them to explode and sink.

Our arrival at Cape Town was met with a joyous parade of locals who mostly never saw any ship even close to the size of the *America*, and they engrossed in the treasured sight with much admiration. While on shore, I again tried making a phone call to Terri, but this time without any success, and the longing to hear the sound of her voice possessed me once more. On our departure, thousands of locals again showed up to say good-bye, this time waving brightly painted banners displaying "God Bless America."

Approaching Subic Bay Naval Base gave me a glance of how abruptly the terrain changed to a jungle wilderness full of lush green mountains and shoreline. In a way, when looking into the distance, it reminded me of a prehistoric setting tens of thousands of years ago with the sounds of dinosaurs in the distance. While the *America* loaded the last of what we needed for Yankee Station, I decided to visit the adjacent town of Olongapo, which was separated by a small bridge and a muddy stream of water beneath. Below, in the muddy stream, there were totally naked young women requesting you throw coins over the side, which some sailors did, and the young women would dive deep into the muddy water to retrieve them. For a moment, just picture that image in your mind, and if it didn't tell you how poor the locals were, nothing would. I would soon find out for myself just how poor this town of Olongapo was and what people would do for money.

As I was walking toward the end of the bridge in my tropical white uniform, a young boy no older than five or six years approached me and asked, "Want your shoes shined, Joe?" All Filipinos referred to GIs as Joe. I said, "No, thanks," and the boy reached into a can and threw a handful of mud on my shoes. I was shocked, as it happened so quickly. I also noticed that my uniform breast pocket was open and picked. The navy tropical white uniform had no pockets to keep cash and only two breast pockets, which were openly visible and easy to be picked. I asked myself how a guy from Brooklyn could let something like that happen. So I reacted to what came naturally and began to run after the young boy when an SP (shore patrol) petty officer grabbed my right shoulder and stopped me in my tracks. He witnessed the event and then explained to me that if I continued chasing after that boy, he would have turned into one of the many alleys of Olongapo, and when I turned the corner, a swinging machete would meet my neck. Machetes were very sharp sword-type blades used by the Filipino people to cut paths through the jungle. That's when I quickly discovered just how poor the people were and what they would do to exist.

The streets of Olongapo were filled with young men soliciting in front of bars and clubs, pushing, selling, and exploiting young women inside each establishment. The temperature was about one hundred degrees, and there was a foul-smelling odor in the air that wouldn't go away. Walking into a bar for a drink to cool off wasn't what these bars were there for, but instead they served as houses of prostitution with live sex shows on stage. To say that Olongapo was a sin city really was truly an understatement. Being hawked and hounded by numerous young women trying to sell themselves as sex slaves was so overwhelming that at one point it became as though I was walking through Dante's Inferno.

We assembled the entire air-wing division with the navy's latest aircraft and departed Subic Bay Naval Base, destined for the Gulf of Tonkin off the coast of North Vietnam. We had the following aircraft assembled for war:

- A-6A Intruder—a subsonic all-weather attack aircraft
- E-2A Hawkeye—eyes of the fleet flying radar system
- A-3B Sky Warrior—attack bomber
- RA-5C Vigilante—swept-wing aerial reconnaissance
- F-4J Phantom—world's fastest-flying fighter in excess of Mach II
- A-7A Corsair II—a subsonic attack aircraft for maximum payload
- UH-2A Seasprite—jet-turbine helicopter having numerous uses
- C-1A Trader—twin-engine aircraft used for mail, cargo, and passengers

Once at Yankee Station, the daily routine became more intense, and serving on the bridge and at the helm gave me the feeling that I was now actually contributing to the war effort. In my eyes, I saw our entire mission as "breaking things and killing the enemy." The C-1A Trader aircraft mostly used for transporting mail and passengers was nicknamed Miss America in January 1968 by the real Miss America herself, Debra Barnes, from Moran, Kansas. Each and every time the C-1A landed on deck, the Miss America song sung by Bert Parks would play over the intercom for the entire crew to hear. I first thought it was a goofy thing to do when at war, but it did work wonders for the morale and sometimes brought a chuckle to the faces of all crew members.

Flight operations were now taking place day and night, and my helm experience was starting to be most of my workday and worknight duties. The bridge watches were about four hours long with a fifteen-minute break in between. During those fifteen-minute breaks, your presence still was needed so you really couldn't leave the bridge but stand at ease off to the side. Smokers were allowed to stand outside the bridge on a tiny catwalk with a window view to keep an eye out if needed inside. Sometimes during the middle of the night, the officer of the deck needed to speak to the captain or admiral. The captain was notified by phone in his living compartment, but the admiral required a messenger to knock on his living compartment door and wake him up. Whoever was on their fifteen-minute break was the person sent to wake up the admiral, and sometimes I was the lucky individual. The admiral's quarters were just down the passageway with a marine always standing guard at his door. I would have to approach the marine and let him know that the admiral's presence was needed on the bridge, and the marine would say OK and I'd knock on the door. The admiral was a deep sleeper, and I would have to knock several times before he'd answer. Sometimes even after three knocks, I'd have to open his door and call out loud, "Admiral, your presence is needed on the bridge." It was during these occasions when the admiral would suddenly waken and begin to yell and curse out loud while making the comment "I'm getting too old for this."

The bombing operations were accelerating, and the *America* was setting records for daily tonnage delivered on enemy targets and supply routes. At this point, there were so many bombs assembled that the mess hall had to be used for storage. The *America* wasn't designed to handle that amount of bomb tonnage, so sitting benches were removed and wheeled carts with three five-hundred-pound, two one-thousand-pound, and even a rare single two-thousand-pound bombs were used for seats as we ate our meals. We were assured that the bombs weren't triggered and it was safe, but it took a while to get used to the fact that we were sitting on live explosives while eating. The mess hall served at the same time breakfast, lunch, and dinner twenty-four hours a day, so depending on your work schedule, there was a meal for your time slot. Having breakfast at midnight and sitting next to someone who was eating lunch were quite common occurrences.

JOE ROSATO

Me somewhere in the gulf of Tonkin

"Freedom is never more than
one generation away from extinction.
We didn't pass it to our children in the
bloodstream it must be fought for, protected,
and handed on for them to do the same."

—Ronald Reagan

CHAPTER 10

—Your time has come to shine.

There were at least five aircraft carriers on Yankee Station at all times, with each carrier on duty for about thirty straight days and being relieved by a replacement carrier for a short break period. During these break periods, the *America* mostly visited Subic Bay Naval Base, but there were two times we didn't. Instead during one rotation cycle, we briefly visited Honk Kong. It was during this port of call that I contracted a serious case of the Hong Kong flu with a fever of 104 and was admitted to sick bay. I stayed under medical care for about five days and lost several pounds and didn't return to a normal routine for another week. On another port of call, we visited Yokosuka, Japan, which is an industrial city about an hour outside of Tokyo by train. The train that ran into Tokyo was somewhat of a surprise for me, and I truly learned train travel in Japan wasn't like traveling in New York City.

I entered the train station and walked down to the track and platform where I noticed attendants in uniform standing under a large black metal frame anchored into the ground. It was summertime, and I was wearing my traditional white navy uniform. When the train came into the station, it aligned the train doors to each black metal frame. It was very crowded, with no standing room left, and me trying to be polite, I let the local people ahead of me before I entered and then stood at the train doorway, facing out, and thought I would back in when the doors closed, just like thousands of other times using this trick in the New York City subway system. As the doors began closing, the attendant standing on the platform quickly went into action and jumped and swung from the metal frame feet first, and I was swiftly double-kicked in the chest, pushing me back into the train and leaving two black footprints on my white uniform. I couldn't continue on to Tokyo because of the way I looked with the two footprints on chest, so I rapidly decided to exit the train and return to the ship without ever visiting Tokyo.

Back on line at Yankee Station, our bombing flights increased continuously during both day and night operations, and so did the Russian opposition by having what they called trawlers parading and crossing into the *America*'s flight paths. These Russian trawlers were nothing but spy boats and radar-jamming vessels disguised as fishing boats, trying to cut off flight ops. An aircraft carrier must always head into the wind during flight ops, which allows planes an unrestricted flow without crosswinds to land or take off. While serving at the helm, I witnessed many occasions when our escort ships were dispatched to intercept a Russian trawler so flight ops wouldn't be disrupted.

Reconnaissance played a very important part in the air war, and the *America* had the best aerial tools available, namely, the RA-5C Vigilante, which had the capability to fly at very high altitudes, uncovering new enemy supply routes. In addition, the navy used the *America* and tested with rave reviews an U-2 spy plane to have the ability to take off from, and land on an aircraft carrier for the first time.

The U-2 was manufactured by Lockheed Aviation and nicknamed Dragon Lady, which was a single-engine ultrahigh altitude reconnaissance aircraft operated by the US Air Force and also flown by the Central Intelligence Agency. It was capable of flying at seventy thousand feet in all-weather intelligence gathering. Early versions of the U-2 involved in several events through the Cold War, being flown over the Soviet Union, China, Cuba, and now Vietnam. In 1960, Gary Powers was shot down in a CIA mission over the Soviet Union by a surface-to-air missile, thus causing an international event.

The major supply route used by the enemy between North and South Vietnam was the Ho Chi Minh Trail, which was mostly located in neighboring Laos. According to the US National Security Agency's official history of the war, the trail system was "one of the great achievements of military engineering of the 20th century." This complicated system of roads and trails were continuously bombed by US forces but were quickly reconstructed and rerouted by the enemy to keep the flow to support their efforts. There were times when reconnaissance pilots would discuss with the captain new supply routes the enemy reconstructed to retain the flow of supplying the south. The captain then would involve the admiral, and a call would be placed to fleet headquarters in Honolulu, describing the evidence, and permission to expand the target area would always be denied. The admiral would roll his eyes as though it was no surprise to him and shake his head while the captain thanked the pilots for their efforts. At this point, I recognized that the war was being micromanaged and saw that the end would not be anywhere near a conclusion unless the rules of engagement were changed.

In September 1968, Yankee Station received a new weapon in its arsenal of ships, and it was called the USS *New Jersey* (BB-62), which was a recommissioned battleship used in WWII and the Korean War. But this time, she had no enemy kamikaze planes or submarine torpedoes or vessels to worry about. Each of the nine sixteen-inch diameter guns of the *New Jersey* was able to deliver a 2,700-pound bomb within forty miles of pinpointed accuracy. At night, while on bridge watches, I witnessed the entire sky lighting up when the *New Jersey* fired her guns. Hearing the roar of repeated explosions from those guns one after another in the distance is something I will never forget. The *New Jersey* caused havoc on the enemy and became the most decorated battleship in US Navy history. There were plans for the navy to bring on another battleship, the USS *Wisconsin*, into Yankee Station, and it was definitely one of the tools used by the United States to end the war.

The next few months passed very quickly, and before I knew it, the *America* was finally homeward bound. The captain addressed the crew on the ship's PA system and thanked all who served on board whether our jobs were as a cook, pipefitter, or mechanic. We all played an important role in fighting this misrepresented war. I knew very well what the captain meant by his words and then reflected on the reporting of CBS anchor Walter Cronkite after his visit to Vietnam during the Tet Offensive in February 1968. Mr. Cronkite's words, at a time when victory was so close to our side, instead gave the enemy reason to think that somehow the USA would not have the resolve to win. I look at it today as why so many died on our side when the entire war could have ended much sooner.

I now began to ask myself some serious questions about the war. How can an enemy be bombed with such forces as the US Air Force B-52s and five navy aircraft carriers and one battleship twenty-four hours a day, seven days a week, and still be a vibrant fighter? Why were the rules of engagement set in the enemy's favor? Why were the target areas so defined and not expanded when requested? If I knew then what I know now, the answer to my questions were always staring me right in the face. The war was run by politicians, which was the answer in all instances.

It was determined that we would cruise from the South China Sea into the Coral Sea while visiting Australia and New Zealand on the voyage home. Continuing on, we would then pass through the South Pacific Ocean and sail around Cape Horn, South America, and head north with a second stop in Rio and a final arrival in Norfolk just before Christmas 1968. This would then complete the *America*'s first voyage circling the world.

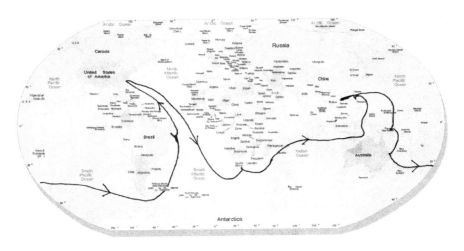

Around the World Map

Leaving Yankee Station and the troubled waters of the Gulf of Tonkin, the *America* was replaced by the aircraft carrier *John F. Kennedy*, which was also making her first tour at Yankee Station. As the *America* started to leave, it was in the early morning hours, just as the sun began to rise over the horizon. There still was a tinge of odor from aviation fuel in the air, giving the smell of war its dominance over otherwise calm waters. The skies were painted pink with very few clouds in sight as I made my way to the fantail (rear of the ship). I found myself gazing at the *America*'s long white foamy wake, pointing and cutting through waves as she was now pointed toward home. These troubled waters of the Gulf of Tonkin wouldn't rest in peace for another seven years.

After our second or third day homeward bound, we encountered another crossing of the equator and once again seized the moment for the traditional Neptunus Rex initiation, but this time, there were fewer pollywogs who became shellbacks. Unknown to anyone in First Division, our leading petty officer James kept a record of who was initiated in the first crossing of the equator. During muster that morning, James called out two names to step forward: one name was Fortner and the other name Bronson. James explained to everyone that these two individuals tried to escape the initiation and thought they could get away without anyone noticing. In Fortner's case, he falsely claimed to have crossed the equator while serving in the air force on another navy ship. James checked his personnel records and found out that he did in fact cross the equator, but it was in an airplane and not on board a navy ship. The air force doesn't hold equator ceremonies while in or after a flight. Bronson was another story, and James explained how he deceptively hid himself in a storage compartment during the first crossing and quickly appeared when it was over to claim the right of a shellback. All of us were shocked that these two guys would do such a thing, and as a group, we decided that they would receive special attention during this initiation. Boatswain mates are not the type of people you want to cross, since most of them are the ship's misfits that other divisions don't want.

After James spoke, we all waited for the announcement to commence the initiation, and while waiting, all shellbacks broke into two groups, affectionately called lynch mobs, one for Fortner and the other for Bronson. Fortner was a small wimpy guy who was from upstate New York and served in the air force for eight years before changing over to the navy. Fortner's military career was not much of anything since he only had an E-3 seaman rank after ten years' total time in service. Bronson was a brawny big guy from the hills of West Virginia and was a coal miner before joining the navy. I was in the Bronson group, which included the worst of the crazies that were shellbacks, and I decided in the beginning to just be a bystander and lie back and observe. The ceremonies started, and the first thing to take place was a large pot being placed over Bronson's head, totally covering it to his shoulders. Another boatswain mate would beat the pot with a wooden mallet while Bronson went through the entire day's ceremonials. At about three-fourth of the way through the initiation, it was noticed that blood was running down Bronson's chest and back since his shirt was ripped off an hour before. The pot was removed, and Bronson's head was filled with blood running down the sides, and he had a dazed look on his face that I will never forget. He was rushed to sick bay, and we were notified that his two eardrums had ruptured, causing the bleeding. Bronson never finished the event, but it was decided he suffered enough, and for Fortner, his lying led him to receive more than his share of bruises, contusions, and welts.

The day after the *America* finished her second equator ceremony, the entire crew went on holiday schedule for the day and held a giant barbeque party on the flight deck sponsored by the USO. The ship's boiler makers took empty steel fifty-five-gallon drums and cut them in half and added catwalk grates to create large cooking pits. There were steaks, burgers, chicken, and ribs, all cooked to perfection, along with corn on the cob and french fries. Music was played over the ship's PA system, and I witnessed a magic moment taking place when the song "Homeward Bound" by Simon and Garfunkel was played. As the lyrics sounded, it brought on a complete moment of silence during the first verse, and all you could hear was the wind passing by. The song was released in 1966, and I remembered hearing it but without paying much attention to it. This time it was very different, since I heard it while being stuffed with steaks as we lay on blankets and stripped down to our skivvies (underwear), sunbathing. That's when the song started, and the moment of silence was broken by a huge sing-along. A few thousand sailors singing that song echoed over the flight deck and down to the hangar bay. It was replayed again and again, over and over, actually bringing tears to many eyes. The entire day turned out to be a special delight for the all the crew, and singing "Homeward Bound" gave us a sense of feeling that home was not so far away after all.

While passing through the Java Sea, which is a small body of water between Indonesia and Bueno, the *America* steamed along in very quiet and shallow waters. There was no sign of life along the passage, when unexpectedly, local natives in cut-out canoes came out of the vegetation growth on various tiny islands and started paddling toward us at a pretty good pace. I happened to be walking through the hangar bay and stopped at one of the elevator ramps to stare at the odd-shaped seascape, when I noticed five or six canoes coming up toward the ship, about fifty or sixty yards off the starboard side. The canoes were close enough to make out the faces of the natives who seemed to be painted in a war-mode design. At this point, the ship began to increase speed, and I assumed the bridge had received warning of just how close they were. Looking out at what appeared to be the front-runner canoe, I noticed that the occupants of the canoe were throwing spears at the *America* as if it were a giant whale that they were trying to kill. By this time, there was a crowd of one hundred or so sailors observing what was going on just off the starboard side, and we all began to laugh at how backward these natives were to think they can spear an aircraft carrier. As we picked up speed and pulled away from the cut-out canoes, within minutes, they were far in the distance and out of sight. The show was quickly over, and the audience broke up and went on to their daily routine.

The night before arriving at Sydney, Australia, the ship's boatswain Hughes went into the forecastle and gathered the First Division gang all together for an announcement. Hughes explained that it was decided we would moor to a buoy in the center of Sydney harbor, just a few hundred yards from the famous amphitheater. Hughes and James went over the plan of detaching one of *America*'s anchors from the chain and attaching it to a giant shackle at the last link of anchor chain. The anchor chain would then be lowered down to a whaleboat at the buoy, and the people on the whaleboat would already have the pin for the shackle. When the chain was lowered to mate with the buoy, the pin for the shackle would be pushed through the hole and locked in place, and *America* would be on display for all Australian citizens to appreciate. Hughes went on to pick the six biggest and strongest member crew of the whaleboat, which included myself. The plan seemed to me a little unassuming since each chain link weighed 490 pounds, and the shackle pin alone weighed 180 pounds. The whaleboat we were going to use was wooden and only sixteen feet in length and would carry Boatswain Hughes and the crew of six and that 180-pound shackle pin. But who was I to question the knowledge of Hughes and James, who both had a total of over forty years of navy experience?

Early the next morning, the *America* sailed into Sydney harbor, and it looked as though everyone who owned a boat was on the water, parading and waving US flags with banners, welcoming us. The six whaleboat crew members and Hughes assembled at a winch station on the forward starboard side, and we loaded the 180-pound shackle pin aboard, and all climbed in while lowering the boat to the water level. The water was very choppy, and the wind was breezy, and when I first stepped aboard the whaleboat, I thought it was too rough to accomplish our mission, but Hughes never said a word. We then rowed the boat toward the bow of the ship and arrived at the buoy and had walkie-talkie contact with the bridge. At this point, Hughes told the six of us that the shackle pin we had aboard was the only one there was and we better not drop it in the drink, because if we did, we shouldn't let go of it and our lives would be hell if we did. The wind began to gust a little stronger, and to me it looked hopeless to continue, but we continued to press on with the plan. Meanwhile, on the flight deck, over one thousand crew members assembled in formation, spelling out in huge letters "Hi Sydney." All this was videotaped by many news helicopters streaming above while capturing the joyous moment for TV viewers who couldn't meet the *America* in person.

The anchor chain was beginning to be lowered, dropping down over our heads, and we kept the bridge fully informed on the perfect position needed so the shackle would rest directly over the buoy so the pin could be pushed through the hole. After many tries and about forty-five minutes of repositioning the ship, we finally had the shackle rested over the buoy at the correct angle. It was now or never for the six of us to pick up the 180-pound pin and place it through the hole while the choppy waters were bouncing the whaleboat up and down like a floating cork in three- to four-foot swells. On our first attempt, we missed the hole and began at least four or five more tries without any success. Hughes then decided we reposition the whaleboat at a different angle, and we carried out his order, and at the next attempt at the new angle, we picked up the pin and completely lost our grip on the pin, and it missed the hole by a foot and went flying into the bay water. Everything got really silent on the whaleboat, and Hughes cried out loud, "You fuckin' losers lost the pin, I can't believe it." All six of us looked at one another with the same belief in mind that we gave it our best, and under the conditions, the mission was almost impossible to complete. Hughes then called up to James, and they both decided a heavy cable wrapped around the shackle might hold in place of the pin. The bridge approved the idea, and a cable was located and dropped to us in the whaleboat, and it required about an hour of making sure the cable didn't have any kinks and they lay in a straight wrap around the shackle. Hughes gave the approval that the buoy was secure, and the ship's engines were then shut down, and we were officially moored.

America's stay at Sydney was for three days, and Hughes decided that the six whaleboat crew members spend four-hour buoy watches in the whaleboat and give fifteen-minute radio interval reports to the bridge during the entire three-day stay, which meant only six hours of liberty on shore for each of us as punishment for dropping the pin. Ferry shuttles were used to get the crew on to the mainland, and the waiting time for each ferry run was thirty minutes. My stay in Sydney was brief but very entertaining. As I walked down the main drag, two young women stopped me and asked where I was from. When they heard I was from New York City, they were extremely interested and had many questions for me to answer. Most of the questions were about how it was living in a city that had Broadway, Times Square, and the Yankees playing baseball. Both young ladies informed me that they were artists and asked me if I would be interested in visiting their workplace. The business turned out to be an animation company that had a cartoon featured in the USA under the name of "King Arthur and His Court." I couldn't resist, so we walked across the street and entered an office building with at least thirty floors and went to the top floor. When the elevator doors opened, I couldn't believe the size or the large number of employees working on animation projects. An announcement was made when we walked in, and everyone stopped what they were doing and came over to meet me, and all were mystified with the fact of me being from New York City.

While looking out the panoramic windows of the office building, I noticed the sky darkening to almost a blackened color, and I said it looked like a storm was brewing in the distance. I was then informed that those dark clouds were not regular clouds at all but instead dust clouds caused by kangaroo herds outside the city limits. It was the dry season, and the kangaroo herds ran amuck during this time of the year, causing dust to settle into every crack and crevice of

Sydney. The office staff were friendlier than could be imagined and didn't want me to leave, but it was time for me to return to the ship since I was given only a six-hour pass for my shore visit. I would have loved to stay longer and learn more about animation, knowing that the entire company was more than happy to take the time out for me, but I had to get back ASAP.

When the shuttle boat I was on arrived back to the *America*, I stepped off and noticed the *Captain's Gig* (yacht assigned to the ship's captain for his personal use) also pulling alongside and the singer Pat Boone stepping aboard for a visit. As he gazed around in disbelief of the enormous size of the *America* from water level, I walked over and introduced myself and shook his hand. Pat Boone then asked me where I was from and explained that he just finished performing in Sydney and was on his way back to the States after his visit. We shook hands again, and he walked off with other VIPs who were all unknown to me.

Our visit to Sydney came to a rapid ending, and as we pulled out of the harbor, I noticed even more boaters on the water than when we first arrived. They were again waving US flags and banners saying "God Bless America" as hundreds of boats followed us out of the harbor. I was now back at the helm and given an order by the officer of the deck to go to a predetermined course. As *America* then turned into the wind and pulled out to the open seas and set our direction for Wellington, New Zealand; Sydney, Australia, became just a speck in the far-off distance.

It was a very short ride to Wellington, New Zealand, and when *America* reached the halfway point the day before arrival in Wellington, Captain Rumble received a phone call. The call was from the mayor of Wellington, and the conversation was upsetting Captain Rumble, who interrupted the mayor and said he was putting the phone call on speaker so the entire bridge staff could hear it. The captain asked the mayor to repeat what he had just said so everyone could hear his request. The mayor once again stated that *America* should not come into Wellington because the whole city would go on strike if we did. The mayor went on to explain that the antiwar movement was in control of public opinion and that he also agreed with their philosophies. The captain put the phone down and looked around the bridge and closely studied the expressions of all the officers and enlisted men standing in complete silence. The mayor started getting impatient and began saying, "Captain, are you there? I need an answer." Captain Rumble replied, "I'm here, Mr. Mayor." Then the mayor told the captain what exactly would happen if we arrived as scheduled:

> No pilot or tug boats to guide us in
> No dock handlers to help moor us to the pier
> No taxi drivers to transport any of the crew
> No stores would be open for sales
> No emergency services available if needed

Captain Rumble gazed out the wall of windows, and it seemed as though he was giving strong thought to what he was about to express to the mayor. The captain's reply was, "Mr. Mayor, we will drop anchor in your harbor and operate our own shuttle boats and walk around your city and safely return to the ship without your help." Then he told the mayor good-bye and hung up. The whole bridge stood still in silence while the captain gave orders to get ready all boats, life rafts, and anything else that floats so each and every crew member can at least step ashore in Wellington. After his orders were acknowledged, the captain then left the bridge, but as he was walking out, applause began to sound, and Captain Rumble turned and gave a big smile then resumed his exit.

The next morning was a day for my division and all boatswain mates to show their stuff. Dropping one of the two 150-ton anchors and extending hundreds of 490-pound links of chain involved lots of manpower and knowledge to safely accomplish the goal. During the operational dropping of the anchor, we did experience a short-lived moment of terror when the chain was unlocked and the anchor was released. What appeared to be a person tangled in the chain went flying by in a rusty, dusty cloud, and the whole procedure had to be halted and the anchor retrieved and placed back into its storage locker. The object tangled in the chain was a ripped jumpsuit with the name Tillman stenciled on it. Tillman was one of the skaters (lazies) who always avoided work whenever possible. James called out for all to hear on the forecastle Tillman's name, but there was no answer. Tillman turned out to be in the head (restroom), hiding from a work detail and apparently placed his jumpsuit on the anchor chain just before the chain was released. James was fit to be tied and got into Tillman's face, and all the division felt the anger that was expressed. The bridge was then notified that all was a go, and dropping the anchor was then completed.

It took two days for all the crew to step ashore as ordered by the captain, and once ashore, there was not very much to do. The city of Wellington was entirely closed for business with the exception of a small tattoo parlor that, as it turned out, was owned by an American who couldn't care less about politics. Late on our second day in Wellington harbor, it was announced that all crew members were safety returned to the ship. The anchor was raised, and without any fanfare whatsoever, the *America* left Wellington harbor. No one came to witness our leaving. I reflected back just a few days earlier while being in neighboring Sydney and tried to compare the jubilant celebration we received just a few hundred miles away with that of Wellington. This was so bizarre to me, especially since New Zealand forces were fighting alongside of US forces in the war against the Vietcong. The only conclusion in my mind was that the antiwar movement had origins in government and the media, which allowed the public to believe whatever they heard whether it was true or not.

Once the *America* was again at sea, Captain Rumble addressed the crew over the ship's PA system and brought into being why he decided to visit Wellington even when they protested. He explained that while being a young pilot aboard the aircraft carrier USS *Lexington* (CV-2) during WWII, he witnessed the brutal Battle of the Coral Sea and the USS *Lexington* losing many shipmates' lives. The *Lexington* was so damaged that she had to be sunk by another US Navy destroyer, eliminating the possibility of capture by the Japanese Navy. Captain Rumble described the fact that the Battle of the Coral Sea was for the US Navy to protect Australia and New Zealand from a massive Japanese invasion, and the people of Wellington owed it to all of us crew members of the *America* to allow a visit. When the crew heard Captain Rumble's clarification, it gave me and many of my shipmates a history lesson while also placing a sense of national pride that still remains in my heart.

Our route home was slightly changed by the captain so that it encompassed passing through the actual combat sites of the Battle of the Coral Sea. I was amazed that over twenty-five years later, sunken ships were still standing up with their bows or sterns humbly protruding out of the waterline as reminders of some of the carnage, now slowly rusting away, all those relic ships now at peace, serving as only a corroding remembrance of that famous battle from May 4 through 8, 1942. Captain Rumble proudly called out the name of each ship and the loss of life count while his voice broke its tone as each ship's name was announced. Among the ship names announced, he came to the USS *Neosho* and had to pause for a moment to gather his composure. Captain Rumble went on to explain that there was the "raft of sixty-eight" survivors who were drifting for nine days after the battle, without food or water. When finally rescued, only four were still alive after all sixty-eight climbed into four life rafts and laced them together. During the next nine days, all but four of these men perished from thirst and exposure; some, nearly delirious, drank seawater and died quickly.

Suddenly, I realized the sun's rays were now shining brilliantly, reflecting off the water's surface without the presence of all birds or sea life. The water was as clear as a swimming pool and had the tones of blue and green sprinkled with shades of light gray. The captain then called for reducing speed to a crawl as we began our very slow passage through the sacred waters. A moment of silence was announced to the crew.

As we all passed in silence with the exception of "Taps" being played by a marine bugler over the PA system, there wasn't a dry eye on the bridge. Trying very hard to stay on course at the helm, I fought the urge but swallowed hard and gave way to the lump in my throat. A familiar voice began to say that these once "troubled waters" were now at peace. It seemed that time itself had healed all the wounds of a war long past. It was one of the most peaceful places I have ever visited, and if there were an afterlife, this would be the place I would want to be. The feeling was as though I was passing over the graves of my loved ones. This entire involvement was one of the most heart-wrenching moments I have ever experienced in my life and still to this day come to tears just recalling the moment that is engraved my memory.

> Yesterday, December 7, 1941, a date which will live in infamy, the United States of America was suddenly and deliberately attacked by naval and air forces of the Empire of Japan. We will gain the inevitable triumph, so help us God.
>
> —Franklin D. Roosevelt

CHAPTER 11

—All your dreams are on their way.

Pressing forward, we sailed across the South Pacific toward the Straits of Magellan, and again we were thousands of miles from any land, with only seagulls and an occasional whale sighting. Forty-eight hours out of Cape Horn, South America, the ship prepared for upcoming turbulent seas. The orders were to tie down everything that could move, which included certain crew members not on duty watch. I was lucky enough to have my duty watch at the helm while passing through the cape, giving me the opportunity of a lifetime. I wasn't disappointed when we arrived. The weather quickly started turning nasty, and the seas began rumbling. A countdown to zero blast-off time was started twelve hours out. As each hour passed, an announcement to the crew was made. With one hour out, a countdown by fifteen-minute intervals was announced, and that's when the bridge crew, looking out into the horizon, saw a bump beginning to appear in the distance and growing larger as the minutes passed. At about fifteen minutes from zero time, the bump took shape, and it turned out to be a wall of water at least forty feet high that we were headed for straight-on. As we approached the wall of water, the ship went into general quarters, which were battle stations for crew members, and all elevator doors were closed. Just as in a Cape Canaveral launch, countdown to blast off the seconds was now announced: ten, nine, eight, seven, six, five, four, three, two, and one. Contact was made, and the entire bow of *America* was engulfed underwater with the flowing water now over the flight deck, and for a brief moment, it appeared to me that the only thing standing out of the water was the conning tower of the ship. The order for all ahead full was broadcasted, and the *America* pushed and cut through the wall of water like a hot knife cutting through butter and, within a minute, safely traversed the famous Cape Horn. Once on the other side of the troubled water, the weather showed nothing but calm seas and sunshine, which I was told is common place while crossing into the Atlantic from the Pacific Ocean.

Shortly after as the ship turned northbound into the South Atlantic Ocean, I happened to be on the forecastle and turned on a portable AM radio. While playing around with the dial, I suddenly started to hear radio broadcasts from the States and turned the dial to 77 WABC radio in New York and couldn't believe that I was receiving their radio waves from such a vast distance away. We had to be thousands of nautical miles from New York City, but over water, I was told that radio waves can travel very long distances, especially at night. So that night, I gathered all my buddies from the New York City area, and we tuned into the Cousin Brucie radio show, and just listening to his voice made us feel as though we were right at home. While listening, not a word was said by anyone since we were all too busy daydreaming about getting home.

Terri's letters kept coming even in such remote places as Cape Horn, and nothing seemed to stop mail call. It was about this time that Terri's letters described my brother, Buster, as getting involved with drugs and hanging around with the wrong people back home. It was hard to picture Buster involved with drugs since he was such a homey kid growing up. Terri informed me that Buster was now living with my father and Pat in New Jersey and had to disappear from the neighborhood due to certain local hoods bashing in his car with baseball bats and steel pipes. The word on the street was that if he showed up at Grandma Rose's house, his life would be in danger. Buster started working with Dad, installing garage doors in new homes for a builder in Somerset County New Jersey, and for the most part, he stayed out of trouble. Buster had worked at a local butcher starting when he was fourteen years old. He quit school as soon as he reached the age of sixteen. When he was eighteen, he already had purchased a VW Beetle and was way ahead of me by owning a car. By the time I left home, he had traded in the VW for a 1966 Mercury Marauder, a big block-engine car and gas guzzler. Reading Terri's letters about Buster led me to believe that there wasn't much I could do, and I hoped for the best since he was now living with Dad and Pat. His new rural New Jersey surroundings were quite different from Brooklyn, and it gave me hope that something good might come about.

Our second visit to Rio de Janeiro was uneventful, and most of the crew felt that being homeward bound took precedence over just another port stop-off. I placed my request for a two-week leave (time off) to take effect on arrival at Norfolk. This time-off period included the Christmas holiday, which I was very excited about because I would be spending it with Terri and my family. When the *America* left Rio and headed northbound, I was called in to see the personnel officer, and all I could think of was that my leave was going to be denied since most crew members preferred Christmas leave over New Year's. Many of the older crew members would be discharged on arrival, but there were still some who had seniority over me. So I kept my fingers crossed and knocked on the office door and walked in. Inside the personnel office, there were five other crew members who were already sitting and waiting. We were told to follow the duty officer to a room and again told to be seated, but this time, we were facing a projection screen, and a video was playing. At this point, I thought to myself that this couldn't be about my leave request, and I felt relieved, but I still had some wild thoughts going through my head about why I was there. The officer began to speak and explained that we six were picked to be the navy's representatives with our local hometown television markets. He then called out six cities, and we were told to raise our hand to acknowledge the city. The first called out was New York, and I raised my hand. Then he followed with Boston, Atlanta, Chicago, Philadelphia, and finally Pittsburgh.

The short video started from the beginning, and it consisted of short segments of what the *America* accomplished while in the Gulf of Tonkin. Most of the film footage was on flight operations, but there were some other subjects, such as sea and replenishments and port visits in Rio, Sydney, and Hong Kong. What really caught my attention about the film was the footage showing *America*'s bombs exploding over the Ho Chi Minch Trail and thinking that I might have sat on one of them in the mess hall while eating and the fact that I helped place the ship inline to carry out these bombing missions. It was further explained to the six of us that interviewing appointments would be made with media management in our respective hometown city during our leave periods, and we would all be spokesmen for the navy. The purpose of the film was to inform the public and understand what the navy's participation in the war was all about. The officer went on to ask the six of us if we accepted the mission, and we all looked at one another, and all replied, "Yes, sir!" He then handed out a large addressed envelope to each of us with the video and descriptive points we needed to know about the film when interviewed. My appointment was on December 19 with the host of the *Today Show*, Hugh Downs, at NBC headquarters at Rockefeller Center, New York, New York.

The day we returned home to conclude our Western Pacific (WestPac) cruise came with marching bands, parades, and thousands of people cheering and waving signs. Among the crowd were some children who were born while their fathers were at sea, and those crew members were given high priority to be the ones to first step ashore. I had a plane ticket in hand that Terri had purchased in advance and was already dressed in uniform, ready to go, when the officer of the deck made the call to those crew members on liberty. It seemed like eternity waiting, but the call was sounded, and I ran down the plank to pier 12, and the feeling of US soil under my feet gave me such chills that my knees almost buckled. Terri and my father-in-law, John, would meet me at Newark Airport in New Jersey, since it was the only nonstop flight via Alleghany Airlines available from Norfolk. John had completely refurbished an apartment for Terri and me to live in while I was overseas, and it would be the first time for me to see it and officially call it home.

Stepping off the plane at Newark Airport, I ran into the first US war protesters I would encounter, and with 75 percent of the passengers aboard being military, it made the flight an attractive target. The demonstrators were in our face, yelling so hard that their saliva was spraying in our faces. The passageways from the gate area were very narrow, and trying to create a safe zone between them and us was impossible. At last I looked ahead and saw that we were coming out to an opening, which turned out to be the luggage area. There were hundreds of people waiting, and the crowd was so thick I walked right by Terri and John without noticing them, and they didn't see me either. My appearance in uniform was a little unrecognizable since I had lost forty-five pounds from the time I left home, and I also had a very healthy tan. Passing completely by the crowd, I turned around and tried a second attempt, but this time, Terri noticed me gazing around and she stepped out directly into my sight, and we then quickly ran together then kissed and embraced. That kiss lasted for several minutes. It was a dream come true. John walked over when the kiss ended and also gave me a big hug and said, "Welcome home, son." It was the first time John called me a son, and it seemed to fill a large void in my life to hear that three-letter word since I hadn't heard it very much in my life.

Terri had decided to take some days off from her work at a large New York law firm, Paul, Weiss, Rifkind, Wharton and Garrison, while I was on leave. During my absence, the Paul Weiss law firm had treated Terri very well and gave her overtime work whenever she wanted it. The company paid her double time besides meals and taxi fare home, but Terri wanted to save as much as possible so she didn't purchase dinners, and John picked her up after work. We spent most of our days off getting reacquainted, and the Christmas season just put the cherry on the cake, making it feel as though I was in heaven. I didn't want to leave. When happy days came along, time seemed to rush on by, and what seemed as a blink of an eye, it was December 19, the day of my interview at NBC.

VOICES OVER TROUBLED WATER

The afternoon of December 16, I put on my uniform and decided to take the subway into Rockefeller Center. I had already studied the package given to me and felt that I was well prepared for any questions about the navy's participation in the Vietnam War. I arrived at the front entrance of the NBC headquarters building on Sixth Avenue and Fiftieth Street then walked into the lobby and asked a guard how to get to the *Today Show*. The guard asked me if I had an appointment. I nodded yes, and I was directed to walk through the full length of the lobby and announce myself at the VIP entrance facing the world-famous ice skating rink at the rear of the building. When I reached the back of the building, I was still a little early, so I decided to step outside and stare at the most famous Christmas tree in the world. While outside, I looked over the small wall and watched the ice skaters gliding along the surface of the ice and heard Christmas carols being played on the PA system. As a native of New York City, certain major landmarks were always taken for granted. I had never been to the top of the Empire State Building or the Stature of Liberty. This was only the second time I stood at the base of the Rockefeller Center tree, and it now had much more meaning to me. Nearby I observed over a thousand people enjoying the holiday season with vendors of all kinds selling their wares, and I couldn't help but think of the war going on at that moment. It was hard to absorb all the festive activities going on while thinking of all those who had already died and also those who were still there fighting in a war nobody seemed to care about.

I regrouped my thoughts and proceeded to walk back into the VIP entrance when another guard standing at a small podium asked me if I had an appointment. He looked down at a sheet of paper and said he would announce my presence and someone would come down to escort me upstairs. Within five minutes, a young attractive female came over and asked if I was the navy representative and gave a little giggle, saying, "Of cause you are you are. You are the only person wearing a navy uniform!" We both chuckled, then we took the elevator without any conversation and reached the floor where I was directed to enter and wait for one of the producers. I handed over the video and was asked if I wanted something to drink—coffee, tea, or water—which I declined. About ten minutes later, a producer entered the room and explained that a makeup person would come in shortly to take the shine off my face and Mr. Hugh Downs would ask me some questions for a few minutes.

The makeup person came in and started her powdering applications and asked where I got such a great tan. I responded with a brief reply, "Vietnam," and heard nothing but silence from her from then on. I was taken into what looked like a studio and sat down in an upholstered chair at a large table opposite another chair. A few minutes later, another producer walked in with Hugh Downs. He introduced us then went into a brief overview of what the interview was going to cover. At this point, the second producer handed me a sheet of paper listing questions that would be covered and asked me if I had any problem with the questions. I quickly read through the listing of questions, and my response was no, but I got the funny feeling that they were just going through the motions since the navy had made the original contact.

Hugh Downs sat down in the chair across me and reached out for a handshake and said that called for quiet on the set. At that point, we began the interview as the producer called for quiet on the set. Meeting Hugh Downs was an honor for me after watching him on TV for years, though in person, his appearance was much shorter than I would have thought. His voice also sounded much deeper in person and more like a radio announcer's voice. The first question was to describe what the *America* did at Yankee Station and how long we were there. The second question covered the bombing missions and whether we lost any pilots or aircraft. The third question called for a description of the crew and the morale situation. Question four asked me if I volunteered and if I would do it again if the occasion came. Number 5 was what I thought of the USA getting involved in a war on the other side of the world, in a country that posed no direct threat to us. The last question threw me for a loop and wanted to know if the civilian death toll caused by bombing meant anything to me. My answer to the last question gave me an opportunity to remind them that enemy forces were fighting US forces from dense jungles and centuries-old tunnels that extended deep into the ground, supplying and giving them cover. I also went into the fact that the targets that were hit weren't civilian and were directed only to military-based or military-supply routes.

Hugh Downs then started to end the interview and thanked me for coming in to the show and for what the navy was doing in the war, and again reached out for a handshake, and the producer declared cut. While Hugh Downs began walking away, the second producer came over to detach the microphone and whispered to me, "They will never play this interview or the video on air. Nevertheless, just in case, tune in on the Monday show, and if it's not played, it will never be." As I left the studio and during the elevator ride down, I kept thinking to myself that this was all a big waste of time, but then again, it was no surprise to me. The next Monday came, and I faithfully sat through the entire show without hearing even a mention of the interview by anyone on the *Today Show*. I wasn't disappointed as much as feeling sorry for the public not getting the chance to see or hear what was said and thus making up their own minds about the war.

My leave came to a rapid end, and before I knew it, I was back in Norfolk, aboard the *America* while she was moored at pier 12. The navy plans were for her to have a short stay in Norfolk and return to the war in a month's time, but the *America* received a bent shaft during the last WestPac cruise, and it had to be repaired. It was decided that the *America* be placed in dry dock at Portsmouth Naval Shipyard just across the Elizabeth River. Moving an aircraft carrier into a dry dock involves precise positioning and takes many hours of tedious maneuvers, and when it's all finished, it possessed a view that not many people get the opportunity to see. When the announcement was made that the ship's position was exact and clear-cut, I then stepped down the gangplank to witness the view. I was completely taken aback that something as large as an aircraft carrier was resting in complete balance on a few concrete blocks, each about the size of the average automobile in what resembled a gargantuan pool that had been drained of all water. The dry dock measured 1,200 feet in length and 600 feet wide while being 100 feet deep, pushing out a displacement of 538,560,000 gallons of water.

Within a week of being in dry dock, the crew was advised that the damage was more severe than thought, and the repairs would take many months instead of weeks. So naval command decided, while in dry dock, *America* be remodeled and updated so she would have the capability to handle the volume of bombs newer aircraft required, thus eliminating future crew members having to sit on bombs in the mess hall. All these changes meant that *America*'s next WestPac cruise wouldn't take place until I would probably be discharged from active duty. It was a blessing that came out of nowhere, and hearing the news meant that I would be able to travel home on weekends for the duration of my active duty.

Traveling home on weekends worked out well for the most part since I had a friend in my division named Dennis Leombruno, who lived in South Glens Falls, New York. Dennis had his parents' 1968 Buick Wildcat convertible with a big cubic-inch engine, and he travelled home every weekend. The Wildcat was a great cruising car with the ability to render luxury and speed with little effort. We worked an arrangement northbound to drop me off in Weehawken, New Jersey, at the foot of the Lincoln tunnel, where I would catch a local bus (a five-minute ride) into the Port Authority Bus Station in Manhattan at the corner of Forty-Second Street and Ninth Avenue. On the southbound ride back to Virginia, Dennis would come into the city to pick me up at 11:00 p.m. Sunday night. There was a certain side entrance of the bus station on Forty-First Street where we met, and we would share the drive through the night and arrive in Portsmouth about 6:00 a.m. each Monday morning, just in time for muster (attendance) at 7:00 a.m. We also had a favorite halfway stopping point in Salisbury, Maryland, at Carol's Hamburgers located on Route 13. Carol's was always opened and was a preferred local eating place that seemed to have a crowd regardless of the time of day.

On the Sunday night of August 17, 1969, I arrived at the Port Authority Bus Station a few minutes before 11:00 p.m. and waited just like any other Sunday night, thinking that Dennis would arrive shortly. But this Sunday night was different, since by midnight, there was no sign of the Wildcat. I waited another hour and still no Dennis, so I figured something must have happened. I called home and woke up Terri and asked if Dennis had called home since it was the only phone number he could reach me on. Terri said that there wasn't any call and asked me what I was going to do about getting back to Portsmouth. I explained that the last bus leaving would depart in ten minutes, and that was my plan. That last bus wouldn't get me into Portsmouth until 9:00 a.m. since it had two stops to make en route. Taking the last bus also meant that I wouldn't arrive at the ship until 9:30 a.m. Being late for muster wasn't anything to fool around with since it was considered AWOL (absent without leave) and punishable at captain's mast. While being a crew member at sea, I witnessed a few who had been punished after captain's mast and certainly didn't want it to happen to me. The marines stationed aboard the *America* were in charge of the brig (jail), and they ran a tight operation of torment and punishment for those who served time in their brig. I boarded that last bus and took a seat in a dark corner and sat down, thinking I might as well get some sleep during the long ride. But I couldn't help thinking about being late and the resulting captain's mast.

The bus's first stop was in State Roads, Delaware, and during the ten-minute stop, I called in to the officer of the deck (OOD) and explained that I was going to be late for muster at 7:00 a.m. The OOD took my name and division, thus reminding me of the consequences of being late. When I finally arrived at Portsmouth, I grabbed a taxi to the *America* in dry dock and had a very long walk from the taxi drop to the OOD, which felt like walking the plank overboard in a pirate movie. Once aboard, I ran to James's office to explain my lateness, and he said that Dennis hadn't arrived yet and the reason for our not connecting was a rock concert in Woodstock, New York, located in the Catskills region that clogged up the all roads in the area including the New York State Thruway, which Dennis used. I then walked into the living compartment to change into my work clothes and heard the compartment TV. The news report showed aerial views of the tiny town of Woodstock with hundreds of thousands of attendees. I saw people totally covered in mud dancing to music I didn't even know and played by performers I had never heard of. The newscast went on about the size of the crowd that unexpectedly showed up without tickets and overran the gates to see and hear the performers. There wasn't even enough food and water for those who attended, and the local police and emergency workers were pushed beyond their limits. It was mentioned that some of the newer artist who performed were Jimmy Hendrix, Joe Cocker, Santana, Janis Joplin, Sly and the Family Stone, Joan Baez, Richie Havens, Crosby Stills Nash & Young, and Jefferson Airplane, to name a few.

The next day just before muster, I noticed that Dennis was standing in the TV room, and I walked over to him. He enlightened me that not only was he caught up in the traffic gridlock but he also attended the concert. He never thought that he would be stuck there for two days before being allowed to escape and return to the ship. At muster that morning, we both had to report to a hearing being held by the executive officer (XO) of the ship in the hangar bay. During our walk through the hangar bay, we figured that we definitely would go to captain's mast. The long walk gave me the impression of being much longer than usual. When we arrived at the gathering spot, the XO began his speech about never ever being late for muster, and if the ship had to leave on short notice, our absence might affect the ship's operations. We were all reminded that a weekend pass only included a 150-mile radius of the ship, and we were all in violation. I was thinking that there were at least two counts against us: AWOL and 150-mile-limit rule instead of just being AWOL. Looking around, I noticed that there were about seventy-five of us being reprimanded by the XO and thought it was too large of a group for the ship's brig to handle and some of us would have to be sent to Norfolk for detention.

The XO began sounding a little less authoritarian toward the end of his speech, and I crossed my fingers while he said that charges were not going to be placed against us since the ship was in dry dock and couldn't move if it wanted to. But he also stated that he would hold this absence in our records for twelve months, but if we all followed the rules in the future, the file would be removed and destroyed. Dennis and I looked at each other and smiled a mile wide, realizing we had dodged a bullet.

In September 1969, while I was on another weekend visit home, Terri announced that she was pregnant and due in March

1970, which confirmed that our first child was going to be born at a naval hospital. There were rumors that my enlistment would be shortened but nothing concrete to count on. The news was a great moment to remember, and Terri's mom and dad were busting out with happiness. The closest naval hospital was St. Albans, where she had already scheduled an appointment for her first visit. It was a clinic-type service and a little unlike what she expected, but the care was very good, and we were on our way to starting a family. We began thinking of names for the new addition and came up with Michele if a girl and John if a boy, who would be named after my father-in-law. When we informed Terri's dad of our choice of John, his eyes started to tear. It was the first time either Terri or I had witnessed such a thing. John smiled and gave us both a hug, and I think he felt ten feet tall that day. He was hoping for a boy, I guess.

Not long after a muster one morning, James announced that the ship's chaplain, Farther Dowd, contacted him and wanted an artistic person to paint a mural on the bulkhead of the forecastle. Religious services were held in the forecastle each Sunday, and there were other murals on the bulkhead but none with a religious theme. Father Dowd had gotten approval from the captain to have the mural painted, but it could only be a copy of a famous painting, *Our Lord of the Sea*, which first appeared in June 1944 during World War II. It was published by the Catholic Church Extension Society's monthly magazine, and Father Dowd had a clear copy to replicate. I immediately volunteered, and James then asked me if I had the know-how to complete the mural so that Father Dowd would approve. I said that I did, and James told me that it was a special request and he didn't want the division to look foolish and again asked if I could really do it, and I again replied yes!

Navy ships don't have many colors of paint available except for gray, black, white, and red so I knew that I needed at least all primary colors, which would allow me to create my own shades of the rainbow. Being instructed to use only colors found on board ship made the task a little more interesting and difficult. I searched the ship from bow to stern and finally found them in an air-wing compartment that was used to repair fuselage damage. I knew that each air-wing squadron had painted logos on their planes, which were very colorful and artistic. It took me five days to locate what I needed, but when I had all the colors, I was finally able to begin painting the mural. I also quickly found out that artist-type paint brushes weren't available, so I improvised by using parts of cut-in brushes that I broke apart and rebanded to be used.

The bulkhead I was going to paint on was painted white, and my instructions were to paint life-size images. The original painting had a sailor helmsman standing at an old classic-style wooden helm, wearing a peacoat with his collars up and a standard white navy-type sailor's hat. The picture also had the wind blowing hard and splashing water in the left-hand corner while behind the helmsman standing upright was the Lord with a glow shining around his head. I sketched the outline with a thin magic marker in an area eight-foot high and four-foot wide and began filling in the spaces with colors as close as I could to the original. All in all, within a few days, the mural was taking shape. I was visited many times by Father Dowd and other officers, including the captain, who stopped and admired my work in progress. In about a total of eight days, the mural was finished, and the unveiling was a great success, with Father Dowd being so impressed that he was lost for words. James then informed me that he and the ship's chaplain owed me a favor and that I could use it anytime I wanted it.

Bulkhead Mural

There were days that I gazed at that mural for many hours at a time and couldn't help but wonder how long it would be displayed on the *America*'s bulkhead. It was a practice to paint over murals, but every now and then, one would be left alone to stand the test of time. Would this be the case for my mural? Would I ever be able to visit my mural once I was discharged? Would future crew members get to enjoy the message in the interpretation of the mural? These were some of the questions that remained in my mind over the years and hopefully would be answered someday.

> Hate war as only a soldier who has lived it can,
> only as one who has seen its brutality, its futility,
> its stupidity.
>
> —Dwight D. Eisenhower

CHAPTER 12

—If you need a friend.

That following weekend, we would be out of dry dock and host a Dependents' Day cruise in Chesapeake Bay by means of a giant celebration with family and friends. I really didn't want to attend the Dependents' Day cruise, so I spoke to James to see if I could have liberty that weekend and visit Terri at home. James explained to me that having the ship leave without a crew member wasn't something he had ever witnessed before, but he would start the process to get approval. I found out later that James went to Father Dowd, who went to the ship's XO, and received approval for me to not attend the cruise. When I heard the good news from James, I immediately called Terri to inform her that I would be home next weekend instead of being on the cruise. As I was astounded, describing what had happened, I sensed something wrong in Terri's voice. She then went on to admit that she and another friend's wife were planning on a surprise visit for the Dependents' Day cruise. Terri also expressed her feelings that she really was looking forward to seeing me on board the *America* since it would be a once-in-a-lifetime event. Terri was then fully into her prenatal care at St. Alban's Naval Hospital. With this our first child and her emotions being very delicate, to say the least, I decided to give up my special liberty and not travel home and instead welcomed Terri aboard the *America*.

The Dependents' Day cruise went well with Terri seeing me in action at the helm. In addition, she had the opportunity to watch me at the sea and anchor detail in the forecastle. Watching the expression on her face while I was at work gave me a special feeling as it all turned out to be a very memorable moment in our lives. It was also enjoyable for me to have her see my mural in person and witness the reaction of all those who stopped by and gave praise. About halfway through the day, I looked at Terri and noticed that she was looking a little green, and I asked her if she were okay. She replied that she wasn't, and I took her to sick bay, which had set up temporary operations in the hangar bay. When we arrived at sick bay, there were roughly fifty other dependents showing the same signs of sea sickness. Terri was issued a cot to lie down on and given saltine crackers to eat, which helped her queasy stomach. I jokingly said to Terri that she was a special person, since out of over six thousand people, she was one of fifty who got seasick on an aircraft carrier in Chesapeake Bay during calm seas. We both became giggly and thought of it as a sick moment that we would always treasure.

Returning from leave over the 1969 Christmas holiday, I walked the plank and requested permission to come aboard as I did a few hundred times before, but this time, it was not the same. The officer of the deck saluted me aboard while a friend who worked in the communications office ran over to me as I approached the hangar bay. His name was Paul Markie, who was from Hartford, Connecticut, and he said that the order had come in from fleet headquarters that *America* would leave for a nine-week training mission in Guantanamo (Gitmo) and she would have exercises to prepare for another WestPac cruise to Vietnam. I responded by saying, "What's good about that?" and Paul said he saved the best for last. His face glowed, and then he said, "All crew members having less than six months' time left [short-timers] would be transferred to base duty in Norfolk and not leave with the ship." Hearing the good news started me thinking for the first time as a husband and future father and what I was going to do with my life. It all came to me in a rush, but I knew that somehow I would prevail if I really gave it some deep thought.

On January 5, 1970, the *America* was preparing to leave, and all the short-timers were called to the officer of the deck and to muster in the hangar bay. There were about three hundred of us who would be stepping off *America* for the last time, and each of us was silent and taking in the moment. The deck officer explained that when we heard our name called, we were to walk to the plank and request permission to go ashore for the last time. Those words sounded as if I were dreaming and somehow I would wake up and it wouldn't be really happening. Finally, I heard my name called, and I stepped forward to request permission to go ashore. I walked halfway down the plank and stopped, then turned around to take my last look at *America* standing high in the water, with all flags flying and crew members waving good-bye. I experienced a sad moment while gazing at her from bow to stern and thought of all those aboard who now had to leave their families behind.

On the pier, there were buses to shuttle the three hundred of us to a receiving station on the other side of the base. There we were told that muster was at 7:00 a.m. and 1:00 p.m. each day, Monday through Friday, and we could do whatever we wanted between musters, with no work details. Included in the announcement was that we would have to stay until our official discharge dates came. It was hard for me to take in wasting all this time for months, and I wondered why the navy was torturing us like that instead of just discharging us ASAP. Most of us hung out at the library and read books. I began reading about investing and how it might help me reach my goals in life. My knowledge of investing was zero, and each book I read gave me a stronger understanding of how Wall Street worked, and I realized that saving and investing were a must for me in the future. By the end of the second week—after reading all the books on investing that the library had on hand—each day was passing slower and slower. So I thought, why not go to the personnel office and find out for myself why I had to hang around, doing nothing, when my pregnant wife needed me home.

I walked into the personnel office and asked a yeoman (clerk) to see the officer in charge, and I was told to make a written request and hand it in. I explained that I served my tour in Vietnam on board the *America* and had a pregnant wife at home who needed me there. The yeoman stated that there was nothing he could do to help me, and I should hand in the request. I shook my head in disgust and began turning around to walk away when a lieutenant called out, "Sailor, wait!" I turned and was motioned by the lieutenant to step over to his desk and take a seat, which I did. He explained that he overheard my conversation with the yeoman and that he would be able to help me. The lieutenant went on about a presidential order that was just ready to be signed by President Nixon. It would allow him to give me orders to report to the Brooklyn Navy Yard's receiving station. He continued to describe what would happen when I got to the Brooklyn Navy Yard and his belief that they would officially discharge me on the spot. I gave the lieutenant all my personal information, and he told me not to mention this to anyone else and be at his desk the next morning at 8:00 a.m., all packed and ready to go. I thanked the lieutenant, walked out of the office, and thought of calling Terri immediately with the good news, but something in the back of my mind told me it wasn't going to happen, so I held off calling home.

That night while I lay in my rack, trying to forget the excitement and get some sleep, I couldn't help but think about what was going to happen and how my life would have a new beginning. Reveille went off at 6:00 a.m. With my dress blue uniform already on a hanger and my sea bag packed, I ran out of the barracks as fast as I could. When one of the guys stopped me and asked where I was going, I replied, "Think I'm going home!" and continued on my mission not to let anyone know about the details. Being that I was so excited, I didn't want to run into anyone I knew and have to explain how I was getting home. Skipping breakfast in the mess hall was a no-brainer. Instead I stopped at a vending machine to pick up a candy bar and soda. I arrived at the personnel office at 7:00 a.m. and placed my sea bag on its side and sat on it while waiting for the lieutenant to make his presence. The hour of waiting seemed to move in slow motion, and I kept thinking that something wasn't going to work out and I wouldn't be on my way home.

The personnel office opened promptly at 8:00 a.m., and I walked in and sat at the lieutenant's side chair with no sign of him in sight. The same yeoman from the day before asked me what I was doing there, and I replied that I had an appointment with the lieutenant. I glared at the wall in front of me and started reading about misconduct and the resulting consequences when I felt a hand on my left shoulder, and a familiar voice said, "I have all you will need to get back to Brooklyn." I then stood up and had direct eye contact and said, "Thank you, sir. I'll never forget what you did for me and my wife." The lieutenant smiled and said, "Have a good life, sailor."

I walked out and stopped at the door to read my orders, which had me report to my destination at 9:00 p.m. that day and even included a Greyhound bus ticket to get there. It was a Friday, and I knew that Greyhound ran shuttle buses to their main terminal from the base, and I grabbed the first one that came along. When I arrived at the main terminal, I called Terri to let her know that I was on my way to the Brooklyn Navy Yard, but I kept the fact that I might get discharged on arrival a secret. I made it her understanding that I would be stationed there until my enlistment was over.

The NYC signs directed me to a bus on the far left in the corner of the building where I was the first to board, and I took the window seat halfway down the aisle on my left, knowing that the view would be more visible from that side. The driver entered the bus and walked down to retrieve my ticket and noticed that it was issued by the navy, and he said, "I don't get many of these." I then told the driver it was my last ride home, and he nodded. "I know the feeling," he said and walked back to his seat. The ride home on US Highway 13 was the same route that I had taken many times before, but it now looked a little different, perhaps because it was my last ride home from Norfolk. Each and every farmhouse and small town along the way made me feel that this country had so much to offer those who were willing to work for it. Passing Carol's Hamburger in Salisbury, Maryland, made my mouth water, and I could even smell the famous broiled burgers and onion rings with the bus windows closed, doing sixty-five miles per hour. Coming on Seaford, Delaware, I recalled a double speed trap that Dennis and I were caught in twice in the same Friday on the way home, and we paid every cent we had for the speeding fines. After that, our route home had to be changed so no toll roads were used since we had not even a dime to spare. The extra miles took hours longer than usual to get home that weekend.

In Dover, Delaware, I switched my seat to the other side of the bus to witness air force Hercules planes coming in to Dover Air Force Base for additional payloads destined to the Vietnam War. Coming into State Roads, Delaware, which was a major stopover point, I got off to grab something to eat. I was entangled into watching many military personnel also changing buses while snatching a bite to eat. I then wondered how many were destined for the war and who would return home. Crossing over the Delaware Memorial Bridge and beholding the partial freezing of the Delaware River brought me back to the contrast of travelling over the bridge during the summer months and viewing the heat waffling over the very same waters. Then exiting the Delaware Bridge while approaching the New Jersey Turnpike brought a calmness that made me feel as though I were coming up on the finishing line and in a safe place. I finally fell asleep.

The sound of bus air brakes startled me awake just as we entered the terminal with the hustle and bustle of Manhattan clearly in my window views. I made my way downstairs to take the subway system and reached the US Navy Receiving Station at about 7:00 p.m. on January 16. Walking into the building, I was greeted by a duty officer of the deck, and I handed him my orders. The officer took a moment to read the orders and raised his voice and said, "Why the hell did they send you here? There's nothing here for you." Since it was a Friday, I was given a weekend pass and told to come back on Monday morning for processing. I thought to myself, *Processing what?* And maybe, just maybe, I would be out soon.

The weekend went by quickly, and the secret was still intact, but I kept thinking of the Yogi Berra saying "It ain't over till it's over." Monday morning I reported back to the receiving station's personnel officer, and he stated that I would be out by the next morning if all went well. He also mentioned that it was his understanding that

Norfolk did what they did because I must have had a really good reason to be released early. I was issued another pass for the day and told to come back in the morning.

Tuesday, January 20, 1970, I once again reported to the personnel department where my discharge orders were ready for signature. The officer signed everything and handed over a large envelope, which gave me a sensation of relief that I would never forget. I was now out of the navy and needed to work on what I was going to do with my life. I had driven my 1968 Karman Ghia in that morning, and the drive home was so filled with anxiety that I didn't remember anything but pulling into a parking spot in front of our apartment building. How I got home I'll never know; it was one big blur. Stepping out of the Ghia, I ran into my father-in-law, John, walking to his house, and he asked me what I was doing there. The cat was out of the bag, and I had to explain that I was discharged. I asked him not to say anything to Terri since I wanted to surprise her that night when she returned from work. He gave me a hug and shook my hand, welcoming me home. As I looked into his face, I could see he knew exactly what it felt like to be home, probably reminding him of his WWII years. I turned and walked to the front stoop and entered the apartment building and heard my kitchen wall phone ringing from the hallway.

Unexpectedly, I was startled from my daydreaming by a buzzing sound getting closer and closer. When I looked up to see what was above, my trained ear as a navy lookout took over. It was a Cessna 206 buzzing northbound over the East River's Troubled Water. As it got closer, I noticed it was equipped with amphibious floats instead of landing gear. The Cessna passed by the United Nations Complex and began to circle around, turning into the wind while quickly reducing altitude. Within a minute and without any effort, the plane glided into the East River. The plane was then in the water with its lights on, then turning toward the United Nations Complex, it slowly pulled alongside a dock, cutting off the engine. This was the first time I ever witnessed a plane land in the East River, and I assumed it was transporting some VIP to a meeting.

I looked at my watch and noticed that I had been daydreaming for over three hours, and it was beginning to get dark as the sun was setting in the west. The temperature was dropping fast, and my cheeks were beginning to freeze, causing my nose to run. My feet were staring to get numb. The lemon-yellow and light-crimson sky seemed to be held back by the skyline of Manhattan. The buildings raised straight up as though they were one giant front gate holding back the failing daylight. As the dark shadows of nightfall began to cross over the East River's Troubled Waters, I noticed darkness engulfing anything in its path.

The old pier planks were shaky as I tried to return over the same path as when entering the pier. The darkness was approaching rapidly and making the trek very difficult to securely maneuver. I realized that I had stayed later than I should have, which was causing me to not recognize my original route on to the pier. With my Sony radio in hand, I tried very hard to keep my balance so as not to fall in. The last thing I wanted to do was fall into the water with no one around to call for help. Looking toward the land side of the pier, I saw what appeared to be a footpath that I hadn't noticed earlier. The footpath zigged lengthwise, and a concrete wall helped me climb and finally step onto stable ground again. I was still a little confused as my mind wasn't yet fully assimilated to my surroundings. I tried to speed up walking back, but I got the feeling I wasn't making any headway. What should have been only a one-block walk now seemed like a mile in slow motion.

Finally making my way back to our apartment building, I stopped at the top of the front stoop, which gave me one last really good view. I looked down Eagle Street where I then turned around to stare at where I had been for the last few hours. A feeling of warmth and complete satisfaction came over me. That's when I knew my future was just beginning, and it would be helped by the past. After all, I made it through those many troubled waters once before. That's when I knew that I would survive what was yet to come. I then decided to only remain temporarily employed at AR Traffic Consultants while beginning an aggressive search for a much better job. I also concluded that losing out on two weeks' promised vacation wasn't the end of the world after all. I started networking with friends and former coworkers and contacting employment agencies, which led me to many employment interviews and opportunities. I was on my way to take the next step in life and knew it was for the better.

Later that same evening, after returning from the pier, Chick and Ronnie were coming over to our apartment for Terri's famous loin of pork dinner and cocktails. This would be the first get-together with Chick and Ronnie since I was discharged from the navy. They arrived about forty-five minutes late, which wasn't unexpected since Chick always ran late whenever we had to meet for something.

Our discussion included many topics of the day but most importantly how Chick and I picked each other as a best man for our weddings. We both mentioned our brothers as candidates but easily came to the conclusion that each of them had their short falls. The true feeling came to both Chick and I that we were as close as brothers, who experienced most of our lives involved together, and it was a no-brainer to be each other's best man. We were both, after all, with each other in most every phase of our young lives. At this point in my life, I felt that both Chick and I had a very special relationship that could only be explained in my mind as fraternal.

In conversation, we also discussed my experiences overseas and especially in Olongapo, Philippines, where Chick seemed to be fascinated about the wild sex shows and prostitution openly sold in all the bars and clubs. Our preferred drink among the four of us was yellow birds, a recipe that Terri had brought back from a trip to the Bahamas before we were married. A yellow bird contained a shot each of rum, Triple Sec, banana liqueur, and orange juice served in a tall frosted glass with a cherry. I mentioned to Chick a new drink called a rusty nail, which was when he started to laugh out loud and also mentioned that he also just ran across the drink. A rusty nail contained 50 percent Drambuie and 50 percent Scotch served poured over ice. I just so happened to have all the ingredients, and it was just another small coincidence of how close our lives were drawn together.

VOICES OVER TROUBLED WATER

I then proposed a toast to our new unborn baby due in just a few weeks as Terri and Ronnie held up their yellow birds while clinking glasses, and with Chick and I tipping our glasses of rusty nails, I said, "May God bless us with a healthy baby. Salute."

> Where we love is home—home that our feet may leave, but not our hearts.
>
> —Oliver Wendell Holmes

CHAPTER 13

—I will ease your mind.

The next two years passed very quickly, and I began working for Robert Hall Clothes at their headquarters on Thirty-Fourth Street between Eighth and Ninth Avenue in Manhattan. The company manufactured and sold through its own national network of stores men's, women's, and children's clothing. I was the assistant traffic manager, second in charge of the distribution of all merchandise from factories and warehouses to their seven-hundred-plus stores. During this time, Terri and I had a baby son named John, who was born on March 5, 1970, only about two months after I was discharged from the navy. My father-in-law, John, was as thrilled as can be to have a grandson who carried his first name. Our son, John, was also the first grandchild on both sides of our families, thus drawing larger-than-life attention and love from all. Being a father for the first time gave me a feeling of purpose that I had never felt before. This meant that somehow I had to reexamine my financial needs and work harder trying to improve the family goals.

Before leaving AR Traffic Consultants, I had become good friends with a coworker named Artie Leby, who was a very talented freight bill auditor. And because we both needed extra income, we decided to establish our own freight bill auditing company while still employed by AR Traffic. We chose the name of Metropolitan Traffic

Consultants, which sounded as though it was a much larger organization. We did not need a place of business since we were going to audit freight bills on a part-time basis at our homes. All we needed was a phone number and address to have customers send their freight bills to. Our small company used a mail-drop service, and we had the distinction of a Fifth Avenue address. Artie's uncle allowed us to have cases of freight bills sent from our customers to his business's warehouse in Brooklyn. The mail-drop service also gave us a prestigious phone number by receiving our phone calls with an operator and made conference rooms available if needed. Metropolitan Traffic Consultants, 507 Fifth Avenue, New York, NY 10017 seemed like a large corporate entity and not a fly-by-night. The auditing business was lucrative, and whatever errors were found, we received 50 percent of the amount. Working on a contingency basis was a normal practice in the auditing business and an easy sell to potential customers. With very little money up front, we were able to get the company rolling. In no time we had a thriving business with a customer base of retailers including F. W. Woolworth, John Wanamaker Department Stores, and McCrory Stores, just to name a few.

Our apartment became a little tight, to say the least, since there were baby items and boxes of freight bills scattered all over the three rooms. With some of the profits from Metropolitan Traffic, Terri and I purchased a single-family three-bedroom home with a full basement in the Sheepshead Bay section of Brooklyn on East Nineteenth Street. We also had our own two-car garage and private patio in the backyard. It was a real nice, family-friendly neighborhood and was just down the street from St. Edmond's Catholic Church and school, which meant a lot to Terri. The elevated Brighton Line subway was just a few blocks to walk and made the commute into Manhattan in only forty-five minutes. We also outgrew our VW Karman Ghia, which had a tiny area behind the front seat that could only hold a small baby carrier. My mother was in the process of trading in her 1969 Chevy II Nova, which was the perfect-size car we needed. We traded vehicles. Mom took possession of the Karman Ghia for trade in, and I received the Chevy II for use as our family car.

Within two weeks after our trade, Mom decided to give the Karman Ghia as a gift to my brother, Buster, who totaled the car in just a few days by crashing it into a utility pole. It was a small miracle that Buster walked away from that accident without injury. The VW Karman Ghia was still in mint condition when I traded and also very well maintained even when I was away from home in the navy. I was taken aback by the fact that he received the car as a gift and destroyed it in such a short time. All those fond feelings of driving that Ghia and Terri posing while leaning against it in a gray chemise dress sparkling in the sunlight, but now the only thing left was an old photo to remind me of those memories.

During this time, Chick and Ronnie lived in an apartment of a two-family house on West Seventh Street just down the block from where Ronnie grew up. Ronnie worked at a furrier on West Thirtieth Street in Manhattan, which, oddly enough, was in the very same building where AR Traffic Consultants was located. Chick transferred from the New York City Transit Police to became a regular New York City policeman (NYPD) and planned on transferring again over to the New York Fire Department (NYFD). When Chick passed the test to become a fireman, he and Ronnie were elated. The change accompanied their recent move to Staten Island and the birth of their first daughter, Karen. All Chick needed to finalize the transfer was his birth certificate, which the fire department required. Thinking it was no problem, he asked his mother (Dolly) for a copy. When he had entered the transit police, she gave him a copy of his baptismal certificate instead, which they accepted as proof of birth. But the NYFD wanted an official birth certificate and wouldn't accept anything else in its place. Chick asked his mom again and again for the birth certificate, and she finally claimed that she couldn't find it. Ronnie, in the meantime, wrote to the New York City Hall of Records and requested an official copy ASAP. After all, it was such a simple little thing holding him in limbo to become a fireman.

One afternoon, Terri and I received a phone call from Ronnie, and she was very upset, with her voice breaking down as she spoke. I couldn't believe what she was trying to explain, so I had to stop her in the middle of the conversation. I said, "Now let's slowly start from the beginning." She then repeated over what I couldn't comprehend the first time. Ronnie clarified that she wrote away for Chick's birth certificate since her mother-in-law, Dolly, kept procrastinating when asked numerous times to hand over the document. When she received the birth certificate from the city, it had some astonishing information that she asked me if I knew about. I told her that I didn't know of any conflicting information about Chick's birth records. Ronnie then went on to say that the records showed that Chick's mother was Rubina Del Prete and his father was Phillip Del Prete. The next question out of Ronnie's mouth was "Is Chick's birth the result of incest?" since the father's name noted on the certificate is my mother's brother, my uncle Curly. This was a question we never would have conceived, much less believed. We kept repeating, "How could this be possible?" Our final conclusion was that it couldn't be, but why would the birth certificate show this outrageous public record?

We knew that no one in the family including my mother would give any true explanation. The Del Prete family had only one person who was responsible and reliable, who would give us the truth and respond to the boatload of questions that needed to be answered. That one person was my aunt Anna. Ronnie and I both agreed she would be the go-to person for finding out the truth. Our phone conversation then ended with having Ronnie to call Aunt Anna and get to the bottom of this confusion and get back to Terri and me with some answers that same day.

After Ronnie's phone call, Terri and I then had a lengthy conversation about what we thought had happened over twenty-seven years since Chick's birth. Each of those talks always came around to what my mother would say when something concerning Chick was discussed, and that was "He's just like the soup." Was that the last name of Chick's paternal father? Was that name Campbell? That was the only soup name we could come up with. The answer to these and other questions we had kept us wondering how such a lie could have been perpetuated for so long without our knowledge. Who else in the family knew the lie? Who was the kingpin in setting up this elaborate family conspiracy?

It wasn't long before Ronnie called back to report on her phone conversation with Aunt Anna. Then I held on tight, preparing for the worst. Aunt Anna clearly explained that her brother Curly was not the father, which was a relief to me. Ronnie continued the story, saying my mother had an affair with another man while my father was serving in WWII and that person's last name was Campbell. Yes, just like the soup. To help save my mother's marriage to my father and the family's reputation, my grandfather Filippo Del Prete (the family patriarch) came up with the idea to have his son Curly and future wife Dolly take in Chick as a baby, while Dolly still lived at home with her parents until they were officially married. They would note the father as Phillip Del Prete. This complicated plan would have never worked or lasted as long as it did without my grandfather's iron-hand rule within the family. My mother was taken to her grandmother's house in Saugerties, New York, to finish out her pregnancy and give birth. Neighbors and family on my father's side would never suspect anything was wrong, especially my father's sister Betty, who worked with my mother during war years. I recalled that my aunt Betty introduced my mother to my father when they were coworkers. The man Campbell probably agreed to an offer he couldn't refuse by my grandfather to never show his face or make contact with anyone in the family as long as he lived.

Those old photos that Chick and I went through many times, showing someone dressed in an army uniform, socializing with family members, now made sense. He was Campbell, the man whom my mother was having an affair with. Whatever Campbell's reason for not serving on the war front during the height of battle still remains a secret. It's assumed that the family treated him as a close friend who was just a lonely GI away from home during the war, because it was the patriotic thing to do at that time. I asked why else would he be in photos sharing family social events. When those photos were taken, no one in the family must have known what was going on between my mother and him, or my grandfather never would have let him stay active with the family.

Things finally started to make sense to me, and I kept flashing back to that night on the bridge over troubled water, when my father said that his sister Betty knew that Mom was fooling around while he was serving in WWII. I'm sure that my aunt Betty wasn't fooled by my mother's long absence from work when she hid while living in Saugerties, New York. The whole nonappearance had to just make Betty even more suspicious of her devotion to my father. Why my father came home to my mother after the war and had three children of his own when he knew she wasn't faithful to him still rests as clandestine. Chick moving downstairs with Grandma Rose after my grandfather died now sounded logical, but the question of my mother having to give up a son and live within close contact for years without showing any emotions still is an unanswered inquiry in my mind.

Up until I received this life-changing revelation that Chick is my brother, I always thought how hard it was for Grandma Rose to raise three children belonging to her daughter. But the number was actually four children who were abandoned by her daughter and dumped on her to love and care for. The fact that my uncle Curly's comments over the years about Chick and me always acting like brothers when we were together now made total sense to me. How did he really feel when those words were spoken? This and other pertinent missing links still have not been answered in my mind and probably never will be.

My mother was a bossy, confrontational person who, over the years, never showed the slightest sign of being thankful to anyone who did so much for her. Think about how my aunt Dolly and uncle Curly really felt about being forced to take in a baby and raise it as their own. Mom would act as though nothing ever happened while thinking of them as just pawns in her life. I now recall the jealous comments my mother made whenever Chick reached a milestone in his life. Getting married, having children, buying a home, or just being successful in life would sadly reflect jealousy in her facial expressions. Then there was Grandma Rose doing what she did for us four children as if it were the only natural thing to do. While all this went on, my mother stood fast while always being argumentative to the people who did so much and wanted so little in return. As a normal person, you would think that she owed so much to those who sacrificed their own journey in life for her. Through my mother's eyes, she owed nothing to anyone.

Chick and I still don't refer to having the same mother, and both of us agree that it's an honor to be called mother, because along with the title, comes responsibility. In Chick's situation, his mother is my aunt Dolly, and nothing can change it, and my uncle Curly is his only father. The unwritten rule between the two of us allows credit to go to those who earned being called mom and dad. This also helps keep the family tree intact while giving all siblings their due.

If this family lie weren't set in stone, would the outcome have been different? The answer is definitely yes, because the truth would not have allowed my parents to stay married, thus Gerry, Buster, and I would never have been born. In Chick's situation, as a best-case scenario, the truth would have made his life hell while growing up with his biological mother and a father who wanted no part of him. Could my grandfather Filippo truly thought this all out and saw a what-if scenario if the truth lived out its sequence in time? Was the family saved by his actions to protect the family's future? The answer is strongly yes, because he saved his family's most prized passion, and that being love. With no regrets—as Mr. Rosiello's rule to always place yourself in the other person's shoes taught me years ago at the David A. Boody night center—if I had been in my grandfather's shoes, I would have done exactly as he did.

During my life I somehow was able to stay focused on the things that meant the most to me while always trying to improve any and all situations. All the events of my life have and will continue to be staged around truthful accountabilities. Thinking back, I now know that sometimes the truth really hurts. But as in my case, I still feel that if I had the chance to make a change in my life, no change would be made.

> "I will always remember and continue to believe that lies are short-lived whereas the truth is timeless."—Joe Rosato

****

EPILOGUE

Continuing in life's journey brings me to a quote of Oscar Wilde: "If you are not too long, I will wait here for you all my life." The things and people in my life that have made a difference are mostly gone now, but the memories still live on.

With no misgivings, my mother, Ruby, and my father, Phil, still are loved and forgiven regardless of their deeds during my young life. My father went on in his life to start a second family with Pat, and they had a daughter named Kelly (my half sister). All my father's shortcomings were avoided in his new family, and the time I spent with them gave me a sense of harmony. My father, Phil Rosato, passed away of natural causes in his sleep in 2008 at the age of eighty-six, and his wife, Pat Rosato, passed away within a year later in 2009 at the young age of only sixty-seven. Both my father and Pat are buried at Calverton National Cemetery. Dad's burial ceremony was very moving, since it was the first time I witnessed a veteran's service at a national cemetery. The sound of "Taps" still rings in my ears, and tears run down my face whenever I recall that emotional moment as I compared it to crossing over the Battle of the Coral Sea in 1968.

The Christmas of 1998 was a strange one, to say the least. Terri, John, Gina, and I traveled to my dad and pat's house in Mastic Beach, New York, for the holiday. Totally unexpectedly, when we walked in, I quickly noticed that my mom and my sister, Gerry, and her family were all present. It was very odd to see both my parents together in the same room, celebrating anything much less the Christmas holiday. I recollected back to when we were kids and never had either one of our parents even place a call on Christmas to check in on how we were doing. The only time before that I can remember them in the same room was my wedding in 1968. When it was time to exchange gifts, I was astonished to see my mom give a blown-up framed copy of their wedding party picture to my dad. He was totally taken aback by the view of his wedding picture after all those years. He called their wedding party a king's wedding. It was also the first time I ever saw the photo, and I counted seven ushers and seven bridesmaids plus a best man and a maid of honor. In the prior years, Terri and I had to lie about spending the Christmas holiday with Dad and Pat since Mom never would accept our attending.

Once my dad opened his framed gift, he remarked that he just found out that my mom was Chick's mom. I was taken aback by the comment, and I looked into my dad's eyes as he said it wasn't right that he took all the blame himself for their failed marriage. He then leaned over and whispered in my ear, "Did you know?" I then nodded yes. This was the next to last time I ever witnessed both my parents together at any family celebration.

My mother, Rubina St. Cyr, passed away in her sleep in December 2000 at the age of seventy-nine. At the time of her death, she wasn't speaking to either me or Terri and apparently had decided to live the remainder of her life without any contact with us. Mom missed out on seeing her great-granddaughter Marissa, my son John's daughter. But most of all, in my opinion, my mother never thought that she ever did anything wrong and took that attitude with her to her grave.

Speaking of my mom's grave, it wasn't until five years after her death that Terri finally talked me into visiting the grave site. I attended her burial day at Rosehill Cemetery in Linden, New Jersey, back in the year 2000 and recalled the general area where she was buried but couldn't find the exact spot. So we then went to the cemetery office to find the exact location. The office person looked up my mom's name in the computer and couldn't find her listing and asked me if I have the correct burial date and name. I did, so the clerk then went into a Rolodex file and suddenly found Mom's location, and with a foolish look on her face, she wrote it down and handed me the paper. I asked the clerk why Mom's listing wasn't in the computer after five years. The clerk then said it was because she had no headstone marked on her grave site, and she shook her head side to side. I became very emotional when I heard those words, especially since I paid my sister, Gerry, half the cost of Mom's final expenses five years prior.

I called my sister, Gerry, when Terri and I got home and asked her why Mom's grave site had no headstone. She gave me a silly excuse that the ground had to be settled, so she waited till it was the right time. In her eyes, five years wasn't enough time, I guess. I then explained that the cemetery already had footings to support headstones in place when Mom was buried. The final comment I made was that the space next to Mom's burial site already had a head stone and that person died only two weeks before Terri and I made our visit. My sister, at that point, promised me that a headstone would be placed on Mom's burial site, and a month later, we revisited Rosehill Cemetery just to confirm it with our own eyes. The headstone was there, and we both rubbed our fingers over her name and said a prayer. I then looked up to the sky and thought of all those years of conflict that could have been avoided. I bowed my head and said, "Mom, may you now rest in peace."

In December 2008, after my father's death, I found myself making sales calls on customers in midtown Manhattan. It was a brisk, chilly day with the sun shining bright, with hardly any clouds in the sky. I decided to drive in that day from New Jersey and leave early to beat the traffic. I ended up making better time than I thought and had about an hour and a half of time to kill. So instead of hanging around a Starbucks, I decided to walk a few blocks east and give the Fifty-Ninth Street Bridge a stopover since it had now been a least well over forty years from my last visit in 1962. It did come to me, with the passing of both my parents, that this would be a good time to turn the page in my life. As I approached the entrance to the bridge, I found completely different surroundings, now highlighted by the Roosevelt Island Tram. The tram now encompassed the entire block facing Second Avenue, including my father's old shop location. All those antique shops facing the bridge were now gone, and especially missing was the coffee shop where my dad had me buy him coffee and treat myself to a pineapple Popsicle. I stood there, facing the tram station and recalled how much better the block looked during those early years. Missing was the special character of each antique shop along with the classic architecture of the early 1900s. The hustle and bustle, moving trams, and stretched cables were now all that was left, as well as hundreds of people walking at a fast pace to catch a taxi or get to work on time.

While taking in all the sounds and views available at the base of the bridge, I turned and faced the entrance again, but this time I proceeded to walk to where I remembered it all started. It took me about fifteen minutes to reach that distinct spot where my brother and I were left off. When I peered over the handrail, I noticed a couple of pigeons standing and looking right at me as though expecting some morsel of food. Paying no attention to the pigeons, I again looked downriver and gazed at the clear visibility, which made me able to see for miles. The sun's rays appeared to get stronger, creating a drastic backdrop for shadows as though they were sharply cut right out of the brightness. That's when the sounds of cooing became louder, and as I turned my head, I noticed there were now well over fifty pigeons perched on and around the steel girders and railings. It looked as though they were waiting for something to happen. I began searching in my mind for that voice to once again ring loud and clear. I began to thank God for his watching over me. I then assembled my life in front of me just like a mirrored image, and when looking at myself, I saw how successful I was. I realized that I could have taken the low road at many turning points, but I didn't because I was given the ability to always have someone in my life for direction.

As the wind whistled through the girders, I heard that voice say, "There is so much more to do." Then as if orchestrated by a higher authority, the pigeons all at once suddenly scatted and left a tumbling flow of feathers dropping like a snowfall. I knew that this visit would probably be the last time I would ever walk the bridge in search of answers. It gave me the feeling that I not only turned a page but also closed the book of my childhood life. I firmly believe that this third visit over Troubled Water was more than a coincidence because I understood it to be a sure sign that my story should someday be told.

Grandma Rose passed away in 1993 at the age of ninety-two, and with her passing came the impression of saying good-bye to a saint. I recall the classic Frank Capra movie *It's a Wonderful Life*, when in the end a little girl says, "Daddy, every time a bell rings, an angel gets her wings." Please make certain that those bells are vigorously sounded and are still ringing in my ears. Just recalling the sound of her voice brings tears to my eyes, and losing her took a chunk out of my heart. Sometimes I still wake at night, hearing the pounding sound of her hot iron pressing my clothes for another day at school. While living under her roof, a day never went by without hearing her say those three simple words: "Grandma loves you."

In 1976, Terri gave birth to our daughter, Gina, giving us the most perfect family a loving couple could ever want. Having a daughter added a different dimension to our family. It brought a softer side to family life while also rendering the need for complete love and devotion. Our home then began to fill with Barbie dolls and toy dishes in addition to John's Hot Wheels and Lego blocks. Life was good, and all problems seemed to be always solved.

In 2001, Terri was diagnosed with breast cancer and was treated by having a lumpectomy, chemo, and radiation. Terri, at this point, promised to stop smoking and gave it a good try, but the addiction and cravings were too much for her to handle. By 2010, she almost passed the mark for being ten years cancer-free and not having the illness affect her daily life very much, or so we thought.

In July 2010, Terri began passing out for no reason, and with each instance, she lost one of her abilities. First, it was the vocal cord, then hearing, then eyesight, and finally equilibrium, all on her left side. Doctors tried and worked very hard to determine the cause. It was finally diagnosed that she had a tumor at the base of her brain and spinal cord. The location of that tumor made it inoperable, and the origin of the cancer was from her throat. It seemed that all we did during these rough times was to visit doctor after doctor without any good results.

Me, Terri, John and Gina

For every wedding anniversary, Terri and I would go out for a celebration. Our forty-third wedding anniversary was sadly a little different. This time we went out, but not for any celebration. Terri was being treated with chemo and radiation once again, but this time for throat cancer, and we were at the University of Pennsylvania Hospital in center city Philadelphia. The last words I ever spoke to Terri were exactly at five minutes after midnight on January 13, 2011, our official forty-third wedding anniversary. She was in the emergency room and couldn't breathe, but for just a slim moment, she regained consciousness. Glancing at the wall clock, I said to her, "Happy anniversary, my love." Then once again, she slipped into unconsciousness. I know she heard me say those words, because I felt her squeeze my hand for her reply as a small river of tears rolled down the side of her face.

The emergency room floor was filled with bloodstained medical gauze, wipes, tubes, and trachea devices. The head nurse then stepped out of the room and left us to some privacy. I stayed at the bedside with Terri for many hours until a room in the intensive care unit (ICU) was available.

For the next three weeks, she remained in the ICU without ever saying a word. There was a day or two that she was able to move her lips, but no sound whatsoever came about. That's when the head ICU doctor decided to induce Terri into a coma after her third day and explained that it was her only chance for survival. John, Gina, and I took shifts and stood at her bedside twenty-four hours a day, seven days a week, hoping that she could find the strength to come out of that coma. The nursing staff couldn't believe in our family's dedication to be at Terri's bedside for this long a period of time.

Terri passed away on February 7, 2011, from complications of throat cancer. My son, John, and daughter, Gina, were with me during Terri's last moment, and we all kept taking turns holding her hands while saying our final good-byes. Never would Terri enjoy the retired life we both planned together and made possible by all those sacrifices during our beginning years together. I immensely miss her wittiness, her sense of humor, and the amazing ability to never complain about any of the pain she experienced. Terri was, after all, not just my wife, lover, mother of our children, but she was also my best friend.

I recall the day or two after Terri's passing when I sat in front of the funeral director, trying to come up with the right words for her obituary. The pressure to come up and write about my wife's life was the last thing on my mind. I was completely lost in the horror of losing my best friend and kept thinking it was all a big bad dream. With the help of John and Gina, we tried to come up with a worthwhile obituary that had to describe an incredible person's lifetime in such a short-pressed period of time. There were so many things that I could have included in that obituary, like her love for cooking, gardening, knitting, reading, bowling, boating, crabbing, and even playing the lottery. For some unknown reason, I avoided mentioning her predictabilities and how much she loved her children and her family. I recall her pointed opinions, like the time she spoke out about how I should always include my parents in our lives regardless of the past. Another time was in 1989 when I was disgusted with my job and wanted to leave and go into a business unrelated to freight logistics. Terri said to me, "If you need to change, stick to what you know best." Her pointed opinion led me to the founding of Aire-Ride Transfer Inc. Looking back, I did the best I could have done given the unexpected circumstances of Terri's passing. I know that her words of wisdom will always remain in my mind and soul in the future.

My uncle Curly (Phillip Del Prete) passed away in 1998 from complications of stomach cancer. His life was a simple one, but it was filled with so much love for his family. The last year or so before his passing, his body was packed with nothing but pain and suffering. During my last visit to see him in his own bed at home, he told me that he really wanted to go so the pain would stop. I was taken aback by his those words while looking into Aunt Dolly's face, which was holding back a flow of tears. After that visit, I sensed the pain showing in his eyes. Feeling completely helpless, I knew the end wasn't far away. He died within two weeks. It was only three years later that my aunt Dolly passed away in her sleep in 2001. Aunt Dolly left a note to her children that read, "Curly, I will now be with you." My aunt Dolly did things at her own pace and did them without expecting gratifications. She did what she did because it was what was needed to be done. My life growing up with Grandma Rose would not have been the same without the help and moral support of Aunt Dolly and Uncle Curly. I will always preserve in my mind those treasured moments of fishing, backyard Sunday dinners, and crabbing trips we enjoyed together. I also remember my uncle's practice of maintaining his cars in mint condition by constantly washing and detailing them and the time he sold his ten-year-old Mercury in 1963 when the car looked as though it just came out of a new-car showroom. To sum it up in simple words, that was who my uncle was.

Losing someone who meant so much to me, for the first time, took place in 1986 when my father-in-law, John Kandybowicz, passed away. John died on the streets of Brooklyn, defending his business. He suffered a massive heart attack while chasing someone who threw a brick through his tavern window. His death was totally unexpected and so sad, to say the least. Looking back at that period of time, my vibes expressed that his immediate family would not be able to cope with the loss. Unfortunately, my premonition was correct, and my mother-in-law's life began its journey into hell. John's son Keith became a drug user and destroyed everything his mother and father built. Large amounts of money were squandered by Keith while he almost depleted everything that was left to John's wife, Virginia. I truly miss those traditional New Year's Eve phone calls from John always expressing that he loved me as his own son. I still think of him every New Year's Eve when I patiently wait for my landline phone to ring at the stroke of midnight, wishing once again to hear his precious words.

Virginia Kandybowicz passed away in 2007 at the age of eighty-one from brain and lung cancer. Terri and I had taken Virginia in to live with us in 2006, since her son Keith used her home as a crack house and totally neglected her, which caused her to lock herself in her bedroom at all times. While living like a prisoner in her own home, her weight dropped dramatically, and her personal hygiene was ignored. The last year of Virginia's life was happy once again for her when she accepted living with Terri and me. Virginia was like a mother to me, and she was the only person that I allowed to call me Joey. Thank you, Virginia, for filling in as my mom.

Aunt Anna (Morelli) is doing well for a ninety-year-old, living in retirement with my uncle Auggie in Long Beach, New York. They have three children, Joseph, Philip, and Annie. She still is an angel in my eyes and the closest thing to the original family saint, my grandma Rose. There isn't a day that passes when I don't recall the love and compassion she had shown me over the years. On my eighteenth birthday, my aunt Anna gave me one of her most treasured items from her first marriage to my namesake, Uncle Joe. She was only left with two of his belongings when he was killed after WWII: an American flag given to her at his burial and a diamond ring she gave him before he left home. I still proudly wear that ring after over fifty years, and I'm always reminded what it stands for whenever the diamond catches bright light or the rays of the sun.

Frank Coppa and I got off track of staying in touch in the 1990s, seeing each other only at our children's weddings. Frank and his wife, Ann, had three children, Michael, Chris, and Peter, who all three became very successful in their own lives. The last time I saw Frank, it was at his son Chris's wedding, and he didn't look too good. When I asked him how he was feeling, he would just say "I'm doing well" and change the subject. Shortly after that wedding, I received a call from Ann Coppa, and she informed me that Frank had passed away. It caught me by total surprise, and she informed me that over the last few years of Frank's life, he was fighting lymphoma and didn't want anyone outside his immediate family to know. He suffered with considerable pain during his last year, and it became his desire to die so the pain would stop. Chick and I decided that we were going to the funeral together, but Mother Nature threw us a curve. The blizzard of February 2010 came along, and on both days of the blizzard, I tried to get to Long Island from New Jersey and Staten Island without even making it out of my driveway. Not being able to say my last good-bye to one of the best people I ever met really hurt me, but somehow life goes on. I will always miss him and reflect about the times we did all those stupid kid things together.

Chick and Ronnie still live in Staten Island with their daughters Karen and Jessica and their families. Chick retired from FDNY in 1987 and began a full-time construction business employing his father, Curly, and other fellow firemen. My uncle Curly truly enjoyed those years working with "the Guys" more than anything in his life and got the chance to get closer to his son. Ronnie received her master's degree from St. John's University and began working for the New York State Department of Education as a vocational counselor for the impaired and is now also retired. Our relationship has seen the many good years along with a few of the bad years and is now stronger than ever while we enjoy getting together often with our small circle of friends and family. Both their support during Terri's fight with cancer provided me the strength to do what had to be done, and I will always love them both for that.

I didn't stay in touch with my brother, Buster, too much, but when I did, it was always at a major family get-together, such as some weddings or funerals. He and his wife, Mary, presently live in New Jersey, and they have a son named Jamie and Richie from Mary's previous marriage. However, there have been events that Buster and his wife have declined to attend. The number 1 event was my father's and Pat's funerals, which Buster snubbed even though I reached out to notify him, and he promised that he would attend but never showed up. My father and Pat took Buster in during his hardcore years, and he owed them both. Just as when we were kids growing up together, our relationship was not very close, it seemed to flow into our adult lives. If Buster ever gets a chance to read this book, I think it may shed a new light on his past while giving him some closure.

 My sister, Gerry, and her husband, Bill, also live in Staten Island and they have two sons, Billy and Anthony, who are married and have their set of children. Gerry is working in her neighborhood Home Depot, and Bill is on disability since his diabetic condition has led to sight problems and kidney problems. I don't stay too much in touch with Gerry, as it seems we see each other only at weddings and funerals. I also hope that my sister gets the chance to read this book since she was too young to know what was going on during those turbulent years. So maybe she will be able to relive those days through my words noted in this memoir, thus filling in any voids in her life.

 My work career started to intensify in 1976, when I became the manager of rates and ratings for the Sperry and Hutchinson Company (S&H Green Stamps) based on Madison Avenue in Manhattan. I was responsible for the movement of all merchandise to their 1,200 stores and distribution centers. In 1980, I left S&H and joined Purolator Oil Filter based in Rahway, New Jersey, where I was the corporate traffic manager. Nineteen eighty-two came around, and I decided to return to the trucking industry and joined Mural Transport of South Brunswick, New Jersey, where I was the director of traffic and sales. This gave me the ability to see the world of logistics for the first time. I then became the vice president of traffic and sales in 1986. In 1990, I left Mural and started my own logistics company named Aire-Ride Transfer Inc. based originally in Freehold, New Jersey, and finally in Manasquan, New Jersey. Owning my own business gave me the ability to control my destiny, and along with my partner, Matt Geiger, I grew the business into a very successful entity. I sold my share of

Aire-Ride Transfer to my partner in 2009 and fully retired and began volunteering as a tour guide at the New Jersey Vietnam Memorial in Holmdel, New Jersey, prior to my retirement in 2007. I also have been speaking at public schools throughout New Jersey on the subject of the Vietnam War while giving students a different viewpoint from the eyes of a noncombat veteran.

USS *America* (CVA-66) was sunk by the Department of Defense in 2003, and with her sinking, all the hopes of former crew members went down with her. The idea of her becoming a museum is over, and it now will never take place. At the 239th birthday ball of the US Navy in 2014, I confirmed with a former crew member and master chief petty officer that my painted mural on the bulkhead in the forecastle was still there when she was sunk. A lifelong question was now finally answered. Amazingly, no one ever painted over my artwork, which was, at the time of sinking, over thirty-four years old. After clearing the ship on his last check for any crew members, the master chief was the last person to step off the *America* just before the sinking in 2003. The master chief also conveyed to me that my speech touched him, and he was proud to meet me. In 2012, the name USS *America* was given to a new class ship LHA-6, and her name will continue to live on.

I owe Mr. Stanley Frankel of Lafayette High School something that I could only say in two words, "Thank you," since I never had the opportunity to ever go back and thank him in person. Mr. Frankel saw something special in me that I didn't know existed, for which I'm sure is the epitome of what teaching is all about. I'm also sure that being the teacher he was, there were many other students helped by him one way or the other.

These are the main people in my life that in some way gave so much and in others took so much. In overview, I find that life treated me well even when taking in the loss of loved ones, but we all must depart sometime, and when I do, I hope to see them all again in a better place.

Wish, hope, and believe…

REFERENCES

Chapter headings writer: Paul Simon
Copyright: Paul Simon Music

ABOUT THE AUTHOR

Joe Rosato is a tour guide at the New Jersey Vietnam Veteran's Memorial Foundation located in Holmdel, NJ. He has volunteered at the memorial since 2007 and is a liaison for volunteers on the Board of Directors. Joe enlisted in the U.S Navy from his hometown of Brooklyn, NY on Dec. 7, 1966. His basic training was at The U.S. Submarine Training Center in New London, CT. He ended his enlistment in the Navy by serving in the Vietnam War at Yankee Station (Gulf Of Tonkin) in 1968 as a Helmsman and Lee Helmsman aboard the aircraft carrier USS America CVA-66.

Joe Rosato is considered a freight logistics expert and has spoken at various trade groups over the years. He is a retired owner and co-founder of his own freight logistics company based in Wall, NJ. He worked in the freight transportation industry for over 43 years before retiring in 2009. He lives in Farmingdale, NJ and has two children. His son and daughter-in law live in nearby Jackson, NJ with their two children. His daughter lives in Silverton, Co.

Joe is an active speaker and volunteer with many veterans groups and for four years also volunteered in The U.S. Coast Guard Auxiliary. He is a lifetime member of Vietnam Veterans of America and holds memberships in The American Legion and Veterans of Foreign Wars. He considers volunteering at the New Jersey Vietnam Veteran's Memorial a passion for giving back some history to the youth of New Jersey.

CPSIA information can be obtained at www.ICGtesting.com
Printed in the USA
BVOW08s1849231215
430918BV00001B/35/P